9 S⟨

to

WIN DEALS

and

INFLUENCE
STAKEHOLDERS

9 SECRETS

to

WIN DEALS

and

INFLUENCE STAKEHOLDERS

A FIELD GUIDE to
B2B NEGOTIATIONS

MARK RAFFAN

Persuasive Publishing

Paperback ISBN: 978-1-7380206-0-7
Ebook ISBN: 978-1-7380206-1-4
Hardcover ISBN: 978-1-7380206-2-1

DEDICATION

For my wife, Jen and my children, Max and Oz.
You mean everything to me.

CONTENTS

INTRODUCTION

"**T**hat's the thing I like about you, John. You're so willing to work with us and you're so collaborative."

John is sitting at a small table in a little restaurant, sharing a meal with the person he'll be negotiating with the very next day. "Would you consider yourself a collaborative person?" continued his companion.

"Oh, thank you," says John, a little surprised by the comment but feeling flattered all the same. "Yes, I do try and always be as collaborative as I can be. We really want to seek a win-win with your organization."

"That's wonderful," says the man across the table, a big smile on his face. "Our negotiations tomorrow should be a breeze then! Let's eat!"

Like most salespeople, John is a people pleaser. It's not a bad thing—it's actually what makes John a natural. He's inclined to help others and is easygoing, which is a great quality. But it's also a quality that can easily be manipulated.

Consider the factors at play in this opening scene: two people are breaking bread before a negotiation. The casualness of the setting and the fact that the negotiations technically hadn't started yet all contribute to a congenial atmosphere. Because of the setting, John didn't realize that the negotiation had already begun.

The next day, John and the counterparty began formal negotiations. By the end of the hour, John had sold consulting services at a massive discount of 27 percent but with slightly better payment terms. He did have to agree to fix any work that wasn't deemed acceptable out of pocket, but the counterparty offered a potential referral to another large company, which could be very lucrative for John. He also received the promise of a great testimonial if the work went well, which would come in handy during negotiations with the company referred.

All in all, John felt great about the deal. Sure, he didn't enter the conversation willing to concede so much on price or to guarantee work, but he did manage to get a few concessions out of the counterparty. And after all, he was being *very* collaborative, working hard to agree on a deal that benefited both parties.

John left the room feeling fantastic—like he really got a "win." He worked hard to get the concessions he received from the counterparty, and he was genuinely proud of his effort.

…But should he have been?

John's Big Mistake

What John didn't realize is that the counterparty had intentionally seeded the idea that he was collaborative over dinner. That seed grew, and by the time John entered the conversation, he was unlikely to do anything to suggest he *wasn't* collaborative (like fighting hard for better terms). John also didn't realize that he got a deal that was totally one-sided (a discount of nearly 30 percent!).

But the counterparty? All he had to do in return was *slightly* improve the payment terms, give a *potential* referral, and *possibly* write a testimonial. John conceded two high-value items, while the counterparty only conceded items that were easy to give away. Not only did he get favorable terms, but he also manufactured a situation where the salesperson felt great about the outcome.

Here's the thing: most salespeople think that their big problem is that they aren't "getting a great deal" on their B2B (business-to-business) negotiations, like John. I know this is true because it's what all my students entering my courses believe, and it's what I used to believe, too. But eventually I realized that my real problem is that I had no clue what I actually wanted from the deal. I had no idea what drivers truly meant success for me, which left me utterly unprepared. In truth, I didn't even know what success looked like. And when you don't know what success looks like for you, you enter a negotiation blind.

John hadn't weighed the discount against what he got in return, which left him vulnerable. It meant that the counterparty could make him believe that what he received was much more valuable than it was. Further, his people-pleasing personality left him open to manipulation. Without clear lines in the sand on deliverables, he was easily convinced into conceding much more than he needed to or should have.

Once you recognize your aspirational goals for the negotiation and the things that actually drive achievement of those goals, you'll never make mistakes like the one John made. That's because in this book we're going to transform your aspirational goals into your success drivers. Using those drivers as your foundation, you'll learn to leverage them to make more money, reduce risk, and achieve consistent results.

Why You're Here and What You'll Get

This book isn't full of cheesy talk tracks to memorize and deploy at your next negotiation. Talk tracks might work some of the time—or during a very specific conversation—but to use them well you must understand who you are, how the world perceives you, and the theory behind why a particular track may (or may not) work in your situation. And if you know all that, you don't need a talk track. I don't think they're very effective or useful unless you understand what it is you're trying to achieve. And when salespeople all over the world start to use the same lines, it broadcasts to the world that your lunch is free to take.

But this book also isn't comprehensive. I can't possibly fit everything you need to know into something that is also deployable in the field. This leads me to my last point: this book isn't dogma.

Some salespeople practice what they learned in negotiation books like they are taking the sacrament. It's rigid and practiced, with no room for experimentation or error. But negotiation practices aren't a religion, and I'm no priest. You may very well disagree with me at some point. And I even encourage you to try other approaches, too, which is why I left a recommended reading list in the back of the book (full of content by authors who agree and disagree with me).

Why would I do such a thing?

Because negotiations aren't gospel, they are a *practice*. Once you understand the fundamentals, there is infinite opportunity for improvisation and expression. There is a natural progression that always leads to improvement, but perfection isn't possible. There's no ceiling. Like learning martial arts, once you become a negotiations ninja, it becomes a lifelong practice.

This field guide is a flexible framework designed for B2B salespeople like you. Each chapter contains a secret and a challenge. Once understood, these secrets will give you the insight to win more deals and influence stakeholders. And if you complete every challenge, you'll close this book ready for your next negotiation.

But why should you trust me at all?

My Secret to Your Success

I am John's counterparty in the opening story. That's right—my background is in procurement, *not* sales. That's why I know firsthand every trick in the trade. I know exactly what you are up against, from every tactic to every vulnerability. I've spent years negotiating deals like the one with John, managing the negotiation to get exactly what I wanted.

But not only have I practiced both sides, I've taught it, too. I'm a published author, I host the *Negotiations Ninja* podcast,

I've been voted in as a Top 10 Negotiations Guru in the world by Global Gurus, and I train Fortune 500 and 100 executives and their teams. Through my training courses at Negotiations Ninja, I've helped thousands of people negotiate better deals and make more money.

I'm on *your* side now. And I've leveraged my experience to create a battle-tested field guide to help you earn more money. By the time you finish reading, I want you to enter your next negotiation with the calm and collected confidence that is usually reserved for those with decades of experience. I don't ever want you to allow yourself to be manipulated into accepting a bad deal. And I want you to know when you have leverage and power (and to recognize when you don't) so that you can enter the room knowing you're rock solid.

I've distilled what I've learned in procurement and sales and transformed it into an easy-to-follow, results-driven framework. If you read the material and complete the challenges at the end of each chapter, I promise you'll enter your next negotiation with the tools you need to exponentially increase your potential.

But to do that, I have to be honest and tell you like it is. I only have a handful of chapters to get you prepared, and that means I don't have time for pleasantries. I can't beat around the bush or use coy language. I promised you results, and that's what you'll get.

And that means that you might not agree with everything I say or how I say it. But the truth is that I'm not interested in making you feel good. I'd be delighted if that was a by-product of this book, but your feelings aren't why I wrote it. What I care about is helping you *make more money*. I can't guarantee you that after reading this you'll increase your commission by 200 percent (although it has happened), or that you'll negotiate like someone who has been in the business for a lifetime (although that's been the experience of my students).

What I can guarantee is that you'll go into your next negotiation with the tools you need to negotiate better deals. Period.

As I've mentioned, we've got a lot of ground to cover very quickly. So grab a pen, write in this book, dog ear the pages you find most helpful, and use this as your battle-tested guide to prepare for your next negotiation.

CHAPTER 1

UNLOCK YOUR SUCCESS DRIVERS

Some salespeople suck at their job. Let's meet one of them. Ben is a salesperson at Blue Sky, a heavy earth-moving company. He just sat down to submit a proposal to a procurement representative at a prospective customer (a commercial real estate development firm). The developer is looking for a company that can prepare a large site for building.

Ben thinks this could be a big opportunity for him. And as a new salesperson, he's really eager to make a good impression. The potential size of the deal is large enough that it could make up 15 percent of the company's annual revenue. He's got his fingers crossed that the developer will sign with their company.

Can you see the dollar signs? He sure can. *Cha-ching!*

When the tense moment arises when he will reveal the proposal, he nervously slides it across the table. The counterparty looks at the first few pages before she asks for some time to review the documents with her team. Ben is worried he's asked for too much, but leaves the negotiation feeling optimistic. He spends the next few days waiting for his cell phone to ring.

Surprisingly, the counterparty calls back within the week.

"You've got a deal," she says. "As long as you can move the start from the first of June to the first of May."

"No problem," he blurts out, barely able to keep his cool. That still gave the company nine months to execute. He just secured the fattest commission of his life. He is ecstatic. "I'll adjust the timeline and send the contract over by the end of today."

He hangs up the phone in disbelief before bragging about the deal to the whole office. That is until he goes to his boss to get her approval on the agreement.

"What's this contract? Is this for the real estate company you told me about three months ago?" she asks, one eyebrow raised.

"Yeah, it's a new deal with the commercial developer I mentioned," he begins. "It's a five-million-dollar contract for twenty structures, curb and gutter—"

She cuts him off before he can finish. "Where is it located?"

He stares at her blankly, wondering why her tone of voice has changed. It's a big contract, shouldn't she be happy?

He tells her the location, and she nods. "And the topography? Any existing structures? What's the soil type?"

Our salesperson is dumbfounded. He was expecting praise, not an interrogation. Over the next half hour, he walks her through the deal.

Toward the end of the conversation, she looks pleased again and he lets his guard down. It looks as though she is going to approve the deal. That's when she pulls the documents out of his hand for a final review.

Her face falls before she asks the next question. "Wait…what's this timeline that I'm reading?!"

"A nine-month timeline—"

"Do you understand what you've just negotiated?" she asks. "We're now on the hook to deliver five acres on six percent grade…but starting in May. You know what happens in the spring?"

He blinks.

"It rains," she says flatly. "We won't even be able to move equipment to the site until mid-June. There's no way in hell this will work." That's when she utters the worst words in sales. "I can't sign this. Renegotiate the deal."

*   *   *

Imagine if the conversation went a little differently. Before the first discussion with the counterparty, Ben sits down with his boss and asks what the organization hopes to get out of the deal.

"What are the most important things you wish to get out of this negotiation?" he might ask. "What are your aspirational goals for the deal?" They uncover what negotiable items are most profitable for Blue Sky Earth Moving's business.

At a high level, he learns what his boss wants (her aspirational goals):

1. To lower risk
2. Utilize unused equipment
3. Increase revenue

Reviewing the organization's goals, he then proposes that the two of them figure out how they can achieve them. This way he knows exactly what he is negotiating for.

He learns that when it comes to risk, the company wants to reduce operational risk. She explains that a major operational risk for the business is contracts that are impossible to fulfill because of environmental factors (like rain, soil type, and topography).

"What other types of risk are you concerned about?"

"Environmental, certainly."

"How can we protect ourselves from environmental risk?"

Over the next hour, Ben continues to ask smart questions that reveal the negotiable objectives of his organization. To his surprise, increasing revenue was just one item of many that they discussed. Figure 1 includes a section of his notes from the conversation.

Blue Sky Earth Moving Aspirational Goals and Success Drivers

Aspirational Goal #1: Reduce risk

- Operational Risk - eg. timeline and control of site

- Legal Risk - eg. liability cap

- Financial Risk - eg. payment terms

- Environmental Risk - eg. existing structure disposal

Aspirational Goal #2: Utilize unused equipment

- Dump trailers

- Skid steers

Aspirational Goal #3: Increase revenue

- Upsell new lines of services being offered

Figure 1

The salesperson and his boss have just uncovered their **aspirational goals** and collective **success drivers** for the deal. Notice that there are a handful of success drivers that are important to the company. Ben just learned there is a lot more to consider than revenue.

It wasn't clear whether Ben was thinking about anything other than revenue in the first negotiation. But if he had mapped out the success drivers of his organization, he would have recognized that the terms he had negotiated increased their operational and environmental risk with a timeline that simply wasn't feasible.

Here is the first secret of negotiations: you aren't getting what you want because you have absolutely no clue what that is. I'm not trying to be mean or contrarian. But the truth is that most people, just like Ben, have no idea what they are actually negotiating *for.*

Secret #1: You aren't getting the results you want because you don't know what you want.

This chapter will teach you how to uncover what your organization truly needs from a negotiation. These success drivers are negotiable objectives that you will use to evaluate the quality of the deal. If Ben had done the exercise, he would have realized that despite the considerable revenue, the deal he negotiated totally sucked.

That's because Ben was winging it.

You Are Probably Winging It

Hollywood has ruined negotiations. We see Jordan Belfort in *The Wolf of Wall Street* just pick up the phone and sweet talk his way into getting investors. And Seth Davis in *Boiler Room* coaching a cold-caller into using seemingly magical sentences to sell newspaper subscriptions. Or Blake in *Glengarry Glen Ross* acting like success comes from being mean to people.

Watch enough movies and you might be convinced that you don't need to complete any prep work, form a clear goal, or conduct follow-up and follow-through. As if the ability to negotiate is some innate trait that some people have and others just don't. Or as if there is a handful of perfect words that if delivered at the right time, in the right order will bend anyone to your will.

Many salespeople believe that negotiations are about what you say and how you say it, rather than good strategy. What happens is they end up sounding wonderful during the negotiation…which is great, but they may end up negotiating for all the wrong things because they didn't have a clear strategy in place. Then their organization will ask them to renegotiate that bad deal they made.

And it's not just Hollywood promoting this idea. So many negotiation experts spend way too much time delivering talk tracks instead of focusing on strategy. Yes, what you say and how you say it matters. But sounding pretty is irrelevant without strategy.

I admit some people are innately better suited to negotiations. But that doesn't mean they don't prepare and doesn't mean that it isn't something that can be learned. When Nelson Mandela sat down to negotiate the future of South Africans, he didn't just plop down in his seat and wing it. So what makes you think you can? Hell, even mob bosses carefully strategize in negotiations. You should, too.

But when I ask my clients what they want out of an upcoming negotiation, nine times out of ten they'll say, "a good deal" or "as much as I can get." As if those statements actually mean something.

At first, this may appear to be a bullish strategy. As in, "I'll take everything they have!" But in practice, it's more like they'll take whatever is offered. And with no clear direction or objectives, there is no way for them to evaluate the outcome.

The best of the best spend much more time preparing than actually negotiating. And yet, most salespeople are just winging it (and may not even realize it). Look for signs that you might be entering negotiations unprepared.

Are You Prepared?

The tricky thing about being unprepared is that if you recognized it, you'd fix the problem immediately. But most salespeople have no idea that they have absolutely no idea.

You might argue, "So what if I'm winging it? I'm getting deals!"

Sure, maybe you are getting deals. But are they any good?

Seriously, are they actually good deals? If you enter a negotiation unprepared—without a clear definition of success—how will you know if you've gotten a good deal? Likely by whether or not you made a commission. But just like the salesperson in the opening story, you can still get a commission and simultaneously negotiate an unsustainable, unfeasible, overall crap deal.

You might make five percent short term, but your company is left with terrible terms that it cannot accommodate. That isn't a good deal—that's a waste of everyone's time. And how long do you think that company is going to keep you on when it appears like all you care about is a commission check? Most of the time no deal is a better outcome than a crappy one.

Understanding Your Aspirational Goals

It's so common for salespeople to enter a negotiation with a loose notion of what they want to get out of the deal, only to later realize that they weren't negotiating for the things that their organization valued the most. They negotiate to achieve higher revenue, but then they discover that their organization values risk reduction more. Or they negotiate for a higher return, but then they discover that the organization values long-term contracts more.

Ben entered the negotiation thinking all he wanted was more money. Which is true, that is what *he* wanted. But when he got it, he soon realized that more money *was not the only thing that* the organization needed. The earth-moving company needed a deal they could deliver on that reduced risk and unused equipment.

Determine What You Really Want to Achieve

What are your aspirational goals for your negotiation? What do you want to gain overall? What do you want to aspire toward? This conversation should start broadly and shouldn't happen in a vacuum. Sit down with whomever you represent in the negotiation. Ask them what they want and what the business wants and needs from the negotiation. Once you develop a list, these become your **aspirational goals**, or the outcomes you want to achieve in your negotiation.

By the way, "getting a good deal" is not a legitimate aspirational goal. Of course we're trying to get a good deal. If we didn't want to get a good deal, we wouldn't be negotiating. What we're trying to do is define the outcomes that make up a good deal. Ask yourself this question: "What constitutes a good deal within the scope of the negotiation?"

Here are a few big aspirational goals you might consider (in both new deals and renewals):

- Maximizing revenue
- Maximizing profit
- Minimizing cost
- Reducing risk
- Optimizing the provision/delivery of goods and services
- Improving working capital
- Improving the relationship

It's okay to make personal aspirational goals along with company aspirational goals. If your goals and those of the company aren't at least related, then your relationship wouldn't exist at all. As a salesperson, you need revenue and the company needs revenue too. However, your personal aspirational goals for the negotiation should never supersede those of the company you represent, otherwise you won't be working in their best interest.

Success Drivers

But once you establish your aspirational goals, how do you negotiate for those items? Since these are outcomes we want to achieve and not things that drive the success of those outcomes, we need to break those aspirational goals down into negotiable objectives. Negotiable objectives are success drivers that will determine the success of the negotiation.

If you're a more experienced salesperson, you might be scoffing at me right now. Thinking something like, *sure, other readers might not understand their success drivers, but I don't make that mistake.* Maybe you're right. And you're welcome to prove me wrong when you fill out the challenge at the end of this chapter. But I'm willing to bet you might just learn that your success drivers aren't as clear as they could be.

(Maybe you'll even realize you've been winging it this whole freaking time.)

If your aspirational goal is to increase revenue, consider what you need to do to make that happen. Will you increase prices, cross-sell more products, increase volume, or get referrals into another part of the business? All of these are success drivers.

Maybe your organization wants to reduce risk. What kind of risk? By how much? And in what area? Reducing overall risk is incredibly vague—you may have a number of 10+ areas of risk to evaluate. Do you want to reduce risk in every category, or in one or two specifically? Why? Further, what is your highest risk area for this negotiation, and where are you exposed?

Whatever you want to achieve, it's important to be specific enough that you can evaluate the deal based on objective enough criteria that you can determine success or failure within a negotiation based on those parameters.

Success drivers need to be solid from the beginning. If they aren't, you'll waver during negotiations. Secondly, they have to be formed without considering what the other side can deliver on. That may sound counterintuitive, and rest assured there will be a time to factor in what the counterparty can reasonably offer. That time just isn't now. (If you realize the counterparty isn't capable of giving you what you need, then perhaps it's time to reevaluate whether the deal should happen at all.)

Forecasting

If formulating your own success drivers isn't complicated enough, you also have to forecast what the success drivers of the counterparty could be.

But how should a salesperson know the counterparty's goals without knowing what they are? Granted, there is no certainty when forecasting for the counterparty. But there are some steps that a salesperson can take to try and understand what the counterparty needs from the negotiation.

First, you can do some research on the company and industry that the counterparty represents (I'll show you how later). By understanding their business model and culture, financial statement, publicly made statements by executives, products or services, and overall goals, you can form an idea of what the other party might be looking for in a negotiation.

You may be wondering, *Why wouldn't I just ask them?* I love where your head's at. I want you to do both. But try to forecast their goals before asking them.

Why?

Because I want you to be as ready for the conversation as you can be before it happens. Remember though, this is just a forecast. We are not saying this is definitely *what* they want, we are only making a prediction as to what they *may* want. We will need to verify whether this prediction is correct later when we talk to them. I'll teach you what to ask and how to ask it later. For now, try to make some predictions based on your research.

Second, you can ask them. This might seem strange or overly straightforward, but there is nothing wrong with being direct. During the negotiation, ask open-ended questions like, "What are your priorities for this negotiation?" or "What outcomes are you hoping to achieve?"

You may have noticed that forecasting takes place before and during the negotiation process. Unlike your success drivers, which must be ironed out well in advance, you'll continuously update your forecasting for the counterparty as you learn more from them. Think of everything that you know about the counterparty as a living document—something that can be edited and revised as you uncover more during your negotiation.

If you aren't entering negotiations as prepared as you should be, don't worry. This next exercise will help you pin down exactly what you want to achieve.

CHALLENGE: Unlock Your Success Drivers

To unlock your success drivers when negotiating with a company, first let's determine the aspirational goals you may have for your very next negotiation. Here are a few common aspirational goals:

- Maximize revenue
- Maximize profit
- Minimize cost
- Reduce risk
- Optimize the provision/delivery of goods and services
- Improve working capital
- Improve the relationship
- Enter a new market
- Enter a new geography

Your goals may be entirely different than the ones listed here. Let's list them out. First, write down the name of the negotiation you will be participating in so you can keep that top of mind. (Remember, each negotiation is unique. What may be listed as aspirational goals in one negotiation may be different than aspirational goals for another negotiation.)

Negotiation Name: [insert negotiation name]

Write two or three aspirational goals you'd like to attain through negotiating with the company.

Your Aspirational Goals:

1. _____

2. _____

3. _____

4. _____

Review what you've written. Can you actively negotiate these aspirational goals? Imagine yourself attempting to negotiate one. What would you say? The truth is we can't negotiate aspirational goals because they are too vague. They're more like desires than specific drivers of success. We need greater specificity. And like all good goal setting exercises, they mean nothing unless you know what you're going to do to try to achieve them.

To create success drivers you can actually negotiate, break down each aspirational goal into its component parts. If your aspirational goal is to make more money, think clearly about what you can negotiate within the deal to achieve that outcome.

Example

Aspirational Goal	Success Drivers
• Increase Revenue	• Increase volume
	• Cross-sell products 2-3 additional products alongside the first product
	• Increase the length of the contract by two years

Figure 2

Do you see how you can separate "increase revenue" into actionable success drivers? Ensure that for whatever goal you wish to achieve, you answer how (as in, how will you achieve it?).

Now it's your turn. But remember, you can't complete this exercise in a vacuum. Talk with your organization to better understand what they need and want out of your next negotiation. Then fill out the charts to unlock your own success drivers.

Aspirational Goals	Success Drivers
Aspirational Goal 1:	
Aspirational Goal 2:	
Aspirational Goal 3:	
Aspirational Goal 4:	
Aspirational Goal 5:	

Figure 3

Now that you and your organization are aligned on your success drivers, it's time to try to predict the counterparty aspirational goals and success drivers. Remember, this is PURELY a prediction. We will try to establish the real aspirational goals and success drivers through the questions we ask the counterparty later on in the book. For now, let's try to predict what we think the counterparty may want to achieve so that we can prepare ourselves for any questions that may pop up from their end.

If you recall, earlier in the chapter we considered all the success drivers of everyone involved, including you as well as the counterparty.

Example

Counterparty Aspirational Goals	Success Drivers
• Meet end of summer construction deadline	• Expedite completion timeline
	• Get highly qualified workers
	• Get extensive and detailed weekly project updates

Figure 4

Now it's your turn to forecast counterparty aspirational goals and success drivers. I understand you won't be able to answer this with complete confidence. But as you'll later learn, making educated guesses is a major part of sales. To the best of your ability, fill out the chart to unlock the counterparty's success drivers.

Counterparty Aspirational Goals	Success Drivers
Aspirational Goal 1:	
Aspirational Goal 2:	
Aspirational Goal 3:	
Aspirational Goal 4:	
Aspirational Goal 5:	

Figure 5

How you approach one negotiation may be completely different than how you approach another. Based on the counterparty, you'll likely need to recalibrate based on different players in the negotiation. This is why it's often best to approach each negotiation independently, thinking of what you may want to achieve out of that single negotiation, rather than trying to apply one approach to each negotiation.

Negotiations Ninja Chapter 1 Breakdown:

Secret #1: You aren't getting the results you want because you don't know what you want.

- Most people do not know what they are actually negotiating for, which can lead to negotiating for all the wrong things.
- Negotiations require good strategy, not just pretty words.
- Aspirational goals must be specific and measurable to evaluate the success of the deal.
- Success drivers must be solid and formed without considering what the other side can deliver on.
- Forecasting for the counterparty's goals can be challenging, but can be achieved by researching the company and industry, asking open-ended questions, and paying attention to their responses and body language.
- Updating and revising success drivers for the counterparty is an ongoing process throughout the negotiation.

Once you create your success drivers, it's time to use them to form a kind of success diagnostic. It's something that is readily and easily deployable in the field and will help you recognize when a deal is right for you (and when it's wrong).

Negotiations aren't a gamble. So up next, we're going to get the numbers on your side to dramatically increase your probability of success.

CHAPTER 2

INCREASE THE PROBABILITY OF SUCCESS

"**I** believe we deserve an eight percent increase," Raj says. He feels confident that he's earned it.

Raj sells operations consulting services to a large insurance company. It's the end of the fiscal year, and he's entered the room ready to renegotiate the consulting deal for the next year. He's spent the last five years working with the counterparty and is starting to feel like they don't value his organization as much as they should. He's determined to get what he wants, or he's ready to walk.

The counterparty is taken aback by his demand. "Eight percent?! That's just not possible." They pause for a moment, considering the options. "We might be able to do two."

"Two percent? *Two*?!" Raj can't believe how disrespectful this counteroffer is, especially from a long-term client. "If you can't give us what we deserve, then this relationship might be over."

"Raj I can't do eight percent," says the counterparty. "It's just not possible. But I might be able to do something less."

"If you don't think we're worth eight," says Raj, "then we're done. Good luck replacing us." He stomps out of the room, closing the door hard behind him.

Later, Raj reflects on the deal. He worries that he took too strong of a stance. But he's confident that the company he represents can't be replaced quickly.

Besides, we're worth eight percent, he thinks. *We deserve it. If they aren't willing to give it to us, they don't deserve to do business with us. They'll call back. They always call back.*

The next week, a coworker tells Raj that she heard that the insurance company replaced the consulting firm with one of the new firms in town.

"When?" asks Raj.

"Three days after talking to you."

Turns out, they didn't call back.

*   *   *

Imagine if Raj had thought seriously and analytically about the best expected and worst acceptable percentage increase he could accept to continue doing the work. What if he managed his emotions better and sat down to rationally evaluate his success drivers from the last chapter? What if this went a different way? Raj may have concluded in his planning that the best expected percent increase is nine percent, and that the worst acceptable he could accept to continue doing the work is four percent. And maybe he targets eight percent as a likely potential target outcome for that success driver.

"I'd like to propose a 10 percent increase," Raj might say. (Notice that Raj asked for more than his best expected increase of nine percent. Always ask for more than your best expected deal.)

"There's no way I can do that," says the counterparty. "But we might be able to do two."

Now, instead of getting upset, Raj responds empathetically. He knows that if he can at least move the needle to four, he'll be successful. So he says, "I understand this may be an unexpected request and may be a challenging conversation to have, but two isn't acceptable to us. What is the highest you can go?"

"Well, it's possible we could go up to four…" Now Raj has momentum, and he can see that the counterparty is willing to negotiate. Over the next half hour, they agree to 5.8 percent. Raj is still disappointed he didn't get to eight, but he still considers the deal successful.

By carefully considering the best outcome he can realistically expect and the worst outcome he can accept to continue doing the work, Raj has uncovered the second secret of negotiations. If you build a range of acceptable outcomes, you give yourself the ability to dramatically increase the number of successful deals you negotiate.

Secret #2: The secret to increasing the probability of success is to create a range of acceptable outcomes for each success driver.

Success Drivers Aren't Binary

At first glance, maybe this secret seems…dubious. Am I telling you to lower your standards so that more deals fit your definition of success? *Sure*, you might think, *it's easy to increase the probability of success if I just lower my expectations!* Here's the thing: I'm not asking you to lower your expectations; I'm asking that you clearly define all the possible outcomes that are acceptable to you. In this way, you broaden your definition of success, giving yourself more room to negotiate an even *better* deal than previously possible.

A binary deal is one where you either get what you ask for, or you walk. Deal or no deal. Raj viewed his success driver as binary. He would either get that number, or the deal was over. This Trumpian-style of negotiation can work…but only in the rare circumstance that you have all the leverage. But most of the time, like Raj, we don't have all the leverage. And frankly, even when you are extremely confident, you can never *absolutely* know that you in fact have all the leverage. Without a crystal ball or telepathic powers, certainty is an illusion. In most deals, a binary negotiation means that when we make a demand and refuse to budge, the counterparty has nowhere to go but out the door.

The best salespeople know that success drivers aren't binary.

While writing this chapter I worked with one of my students to increase her probability of success during a renewal negotiation. I began by asking her to show me her drivers. One was to increase the revenue of the deal by seven percent.

"Let's look at your revenue driver," I said. "How will you feel about the deal if you don't get seven?"

"I'll feel like I totally bombed," she said. "It would be awful."

"What happens if you get 6.8?"

"Well, that would still be good," she responded.

"What if you get four? Would you have failed then?" I asked.

"I don't know," she said, taking the time to really consider what that would mean for her career. "I guess not. It's still good."

"That's a wide range between seven and four," I observed. "At what percentage would you not accept the deal?"

After some reflection, she determined that even at a zero percent increase, she would still like to renew the contract, as it was already quite profitable for her.

"Then even if nothing changes," I told her, "you'd still be successful because it would still be a good deal, right?"

"Yes, I think so."

"What would it take for you to not renew the contract?" I asked.

"A decrease, I suppose."

Let's reflect on what just happened. My student began this conversation believing that any outcome less than a seven percent increase would be a complete failure. An absolute nonstarter. It would mean that she totally failed. But by the end of our conversation, she realized that the only actual failure would be a decrease. That's a wildly different definition of success, isn't it?

Many high performers like the student in the previous story think in binary terms. It seems to be a by-product of challenging yourself with high expectations. They set high goals—which is wonderful—but if they don't meet or exceed them completely, they feel as though they have failed. The problem with this mindset is that it leads to situations like Raj's, where if they don't get exactly what they asked for, they often consider it a failure. If Raj could have realized what my student did, maybe he could have stood a chance to negotiate a good deal for himself.

You might try to argue that my student is lowering her standards. But in practice she has done anything but. Once she enters negotiations, she will still negotiate to try to achieve the top of her range. There is no rule that states one must negotiate to the bottom. On the contrary, the reason we set the range of acceptable outcomes is to give yourself a benchmark to make sure that you don't negotiate below your worst acceptable deal into a bad deal. But by doing the exercise, she gave herself room to move during a negotiation. Now she won't lose out on a profitable deal because she was unwilling to budge on terms.

So how do you create a range? And how do you determine the top and bottom of that range? This next section will teach you how to uncover both ends of the spectrum of a profitable deal.

Define Your Range of Acceptable Outcomes

To build a range of acceptable outcomes for your success drivers, you must determine three key items: the best expected outcome, target outcome, and worst acceptable outcome. It's important to realize that the range you create with the best expected, target, and worst acceptable deal are influenced by the market conditions, the industry, the geography, and the competition in the industry. Also, these outcomes are based on each success driver, not the deal as a whole. I'll explain why soon, but for now, understand that it's critical to map out a range for each driver independently.

The **target outcome** is where you think the deal is likely going to land. This outcome should be based on market research, historical data, forecasted data, and your own experience. With everything you know about the counterparty, your product, the competition, and any other factors, what is the most likely outcome for this specific success driver? The target may not be in the middle of your best expected outcome and worst acceptable outcomes. Based on what you know, you may place this metric closer to the worst acceptable or best expected outcome.

The **best expected outcome** is the best you could achieve within the realm of possibility. Is it possible to increase the price by 70 percent? Maybe not. But 15 percent? Maybe, depending on your industry and the service or product you provide. The best expected outcome should reflect the best possible deal you could expect within the realm of possibility given the current market, geography, and industry.

The **worst acceptable outcome** is the point right *before* you walk away from the deal. What is the worst situation in which the deal would still make sense for you? At what point would you leave? When would the deal no longer be profitable for your organization? This is perhaps the most important point on your range of acceptable outcomes.

Some salespeople never map out the worst acceptable outcome because they feel like if they define it, then they will always negotiate to the bottom. As if simply considering the worst acceptable scenario makes it a self-fulfilling prophecy. I don't think ignoring the worst acceptable outcome is necessarily an intentional strategy, but instead a subconscious response. Like a college student ignoring the dishes in the sink until their apartment stinks. Juvenile, maybe—but also very human. If I don't see or acknowledge the danger, is it really there?

Yes, of course it is!

Ignoring the fact that the deal could go sideways doesn't mean it magically won't. That's just delusional. But by drawing a line in the sand you're unwilling to cross, you protect yourself from being persuaded or coerced into accepting a deal that doesn't work for you. When you know *exactly* what is unacceptable, you ensure you never accept a deal that exposes you to too much risk, is unprofitable, or builds a relationship set on an unfavorable precedent.

Consider what a massive gift that is to give yourself. If you know specifically what you won't accept, then you protect yourself from ever negotiating a bad deal again. You'll never have to explain to your boss why you exposed the company to a huge amount of liability. Or why the terms are terrible. Or be asked to renegotiate the deal. All that, simply by having the foresight to clearly define what you will not accept.

That's a pretty damn good return on your time, if you ask me.

So let's build a range of acceptable outcomes that will help you dodge bad deals for the rest of your career.

Build Your Success Framework

Imagine these are your success drivers for a contract renewal:

- Aspirational Goal: Increase revenue
  - Success driver #1: Increase prices
- Aspirational Goal: Increase working capital
  - Success driver #2: Improve payment terms
- Aspirational Goal: Improve length of agreement
  - Success driver #3: Improve the relationship

The challenge now is to define the target outcome, worst acceptable outcome, and best expected outcome for each.

Let's start with success driver #1: increase prices.

Based on your research and experience, you determine that your target price increase is five percent. This is the outcome that you think is most likely for this specific success driver. Within the realm of possibility, you decide that nine percent is the best expected outcome. You also determine that the current contract does not meet your organization's needs, and therefore you must at least meet an increase of three percent to continue performing the work. This is your worst acceptable outcome.

Following the same procedure for success driver #2, you determine your target outcome is 45 days, the worst acceptable outcome is 90 days, and the best expected outcome is 15 days.

Success driver #3 is a little less straightforward than the other two. Namely, because it forces you to objectively measure something somewhat subjective, like the health of a relationship. However, there are metrics you can use to evaluate subjective success drivers—it'll just take some creative thinking.

To improve a relationship, you first need an accurate under-standing of what that relationship currently looks like. Then, consider where you want to be. Next, how will you get there? A monthly lunch? Quarterly business reviews? A round of golf? It could also be something more objective, like an improved net promoter score. In this scenario, you decide the target out-come is a monthly meeting, the worst acceptable outcome is no change whatsoever, and the best expected outcome is a quarterly review over dinner and a monthly meeting.

With your range defined for each outcome, you can now cre-ate a **success framework**. A success framework is a way to organize the range of acceptable outcomes and success drivers to give you a clear map of every successful outcome of a deal.

Success Framework

Success Drivers	Worst Acceptable Outcome	Target Outcome	Best Expected Outcome
Increase Prices	3%	5%	9%
Better Payment Terms	90 days	45 days	15 days
Improve Relationship	No change	Monthly Meeting	Quarterly review over dinner and monthly meeting

Figure 6

When evaluating your target and best expected outcome, you may wonder how specific to make your answers. For example, if you have a list of ten products you sell, do you need to create a high and low price for each? Not necessarily. Instead, conduct a separate pricing analysis to determine a weighted average increase and make that your best outcome for the price driver.

When it comes to the worst acceptable outcome, it's wise to be specific enough that you'll recognize when the counterparty crosses the threshold into nonnegotiable territory. For example, knowing you absolutely won't accept terms longer than 90 days is much more helpful than loosely deciding that anything over 100 might not be worth it. Make sure that you define a worst acceptable outcome that you will be able to recognize in the heat of the moment.

As a friendly reminder, none of this planning should happen in a vacuum. Work with whomever you represent or whomever the decision-maker is internally within your business to determine what the range of acceptable outcomes are for each success driver.

Bartering Your Success Drivers

When reflecting on outcomes, my students will often start negotiating each success driver prematurely. They'll tell me something like, "Well, maybe I'd accept a lower price if I got better payment terms." Your head is in the right place, but we're not there yet.

The point of this exercise is to understand first what the bottom end of the range looks like for each success driver, *individually*. Once you understand each term on its own, then you can determine which success drivers are tradeable against each other (and at what price point, percentage, etc.). Without individual evaluation, it's difficult to fully appreciate what can and cannot be done within the deal.

Building a range of acceptable outcomes for each success driver can help you bargain on an individual term, like price. Say you want something for fifty dollars, but I want it for eighty dollars. Your worst acceptable outcome is paying seventy dollars, so you now have room in your negotiation to settle on price. But having a range also helps when bartering. Maybe you're willing to accept less for item one as long as you get more of item two. For example, perhaps you'd be willing to accept charging a lower price if you got better payment terms.

Once you can identify the range of acceptable outcomes for each success driver, you can readily propose alternatives to the counterparty in the event they ask for something that you may not be able to give. Thinking back to the opening story, what if Raj accepted a five percent increase (instead of eight) as long as the company was willing to extend the contract by another year? That sounds like a pretty good deal to me.

What if the Counterparty Doesn't Fit in Your Range?

Even the best negotiators find themselves negotiating with a counterparty that does not fit into the range of acceptable outcomes of their most important success drivers. Sooner or later, it will happen, so it's a good idea to consider how you'll respond ahead of time.

If the counterparty won't at the very least meet your worst acceptable outcome of your most important success drivers, you now must have a serious conversation with someone internally within your business who has the decision-making authority to make a call on the deal. In this situation, there are three questions you must ask them:

1. Do you want to change what you're willing to accept?
2. Can you help me negotiate the counterparty back into range?
3. Do you want to walk away from this deal?

In the event you're instructed to walk away, do yourself a favor and get it in writing. Any miscommunication could lead to you being blamed for walking away from a significant deal.

CHALLENGE: Build Your Success Framework

Now that you understand how to create a range of acceptable outcomes for your success drivers, it's time to build your own. To do so, you'll determine the worst acceptable deal, target deal, and best expected deal for the list of prioritized success drivers from Chapter 1.

Determine your worst acceptable, best expected, and target outcome.

Example

Success Drivers	Worst Acceptable Outcome	Target Outcome	Best Expected Outcome
Increase Prices	3%	5%	9%
Better Payment Terms	90 days	45 days	15 days
Improve Relationship	No change	Monthly Meeting	Quarterly review over dinner and monthly meeting

Figure 7

Fill out the empty fields in Figure 8 to uncover your worst, best, and target outcomes for each of your success drivers that you created in Chapter 1.

Success Drivers	Worst Acceptable Outcome	Target Outcome	Best Expected Outcome

Figure 8

Use your success framework as a deployable map in the field. Print one out for each negotiation and have it with you in the room. Use it to ensure you never accept a bad deal, and to identify which success drivers are tradeable against each other and at what price point or percentage.

Negotiations Ninja Chapter 2 Breakdown

Secret #2: The secret to increasing the probability of success is to create a range of acceptable outcomes for each success driver.

- Binary negotiations can lead to situations where if you don't get exactly what you asked for, you might pull the nuclear option on an otherwise profitable deal.

- Success drivers are not binary; rather, you should define a range of acceptable outcomes to broaden your definition of success.

- To build a range of acceptable outcomes for your success drivers, you must determine three key items: the best expected outcome, target outcome, and worst acceptable outcome.

- Deploy your success framework in the field and use it to steer clear of bad deals and identify tradeable items.

With success drivers defined and a success framework in hand, you're ready to move into a territory that you may have never considered. At first, this next chapter might seem counterintuitive and counterproductive. But stick with me because coming up next is one of the most critical skills of any salesperson.

It's time to win by choosing what you might be willing to lose.

WIN BY CHOOSING WHAT YOU MIGHT BE WILLING TO LOSE

"**A**re you ready to make a deal today?" Maria asks, hoping the counterparty can't hear the desperation in her voice. She needed this deal to go through months ago.

"I think we can work something out," he says.

Maria sighs in relief. They had been stringing her along since June, with the last quarter having recently arrived and disappearing fast. Just last week, her boss asked why she hadn't met her quota, and she assured him that she'd make it up by the end of the year. This was a million-dollar contract, and she was certain that if she could just get the counterparty to sign, she'd be in the clear.

"We're still considering our options," says the counterparty. "And we've looked at the competition. Have you heard about that new company, Privacy Force? They've been really competitive in the market. Fascinating stuff. Really cutting edge and such great value…"

"Well, we do offer some benefits that they don't—"

"Look, I think we can make this work if you can take off 10 percent. Otherwise we'll need to reevaluate our options."

She hasn't gone into the negotiation willing to give up that much. But despite the discount, Maria is relieved, knowing that she's been cleared to discount up to twelve. She briefly considers further negotiating the deal, but the thought leaves as quickly as it comes. She needs this deal to go through, and she can't risk something going wrong while arguing terms. The deal must happen today.

"Yes, absolutely," she blurts out, "I'll write up the contract and send it over today."

*   *   *

Maria ends up with a signed contract and a fat commission. And the consulting company she represents makes a significant deal.

How could I possibly find fault with that?

For one, Maria never should have given away something without asking for something in return. She left a massive amount of opportunity on the table by effectively gifting that company $100,000 *without receiving anything in return*. Imagine all the different success drivers Maria could have negotiated in exchange for the discount, like payment terms, contract length, a smaller discount, a cross-sale, or even an agreement to use their software across multiple sites.

She could have negotiated any one of those terms and easily improved the deal, but instead chose to close.

And what is the counterparty supposed to think of this gift? If Maria was so willing to give away 10 percent, maybe she'll concede even more in the future. By not countering, Maria left herself vulnerable for future negotiations. She just set the expectation that the counterparty can bleed her dry at the end of every fiscal year. That doesn't sound like a good working relationship, does it?

From my years working in procurement, I know exactly how the counterparty maneuvered Maria into this deal. You see, the counterparty knew that many sales reps have quarterly or annual sales targets, and therefore recognized that the best way to get a discount on the product was to wait out the clock. If they could push the deal out toward the end of the fiscal year, they knew she would be more likely to agree to their demands. They had a lot of leverage.

Part of why the counterparty's strategy was so effective is that Maria felt like she had to expedite the deal. When someone really wants a deal to go through, they'll say just about anything to get a signed contract as soon as possible.

There doesn't have to be a sales quota looming in the background for this type of behavior to occur. I've listened to sales calls before where the customer asks for a discount or some other benefit, and as long as it's within their approval authority, the salesperson simply agrees to the request without asking for anything in return.

It sounds something like, "Can you knock off 10 percent?"

"Yes! You betcha," and they shake hands.

Meanwhile I'm on the sidelines, thinking, *WOAH, SLOW DOWN! YOU JUST AGREED TO CUT THE PRICE OF A MULTIMILLION DOLLAR DEAL BY 10 PERCENT. THAT'S HUNDREDS OF THOUSANDS OF DOLLARS!!!*

I recognize that I'm generalizing, but most salespeople automatically say "yes" to any request. They want to make their customers happy and avoid conflict whenever possible. That's part of why they are so great at sales—they are likable and willing to work hard on behalf of others. But any desire to please must be tempered with a smart concession strategy already in place.

What if Maria was able to concede more carefully based on a well-planned approach? The counterparty would have asked for 10 percent, and she might have responded, "I might be able to do three, if we can discuss reducing payment terms to net 45 from net 90."

"That's not possible," the counterparty might say. "We'd need at least five percent to offer those kinds of payment terms."

"I think we could do that deal," Maria says.

And both parties agree to a deal.

In this scenario, Maria got the client to agree to a five percent discount with payment terms of 45 days. Despite being in a vulnerable position due to the timeline, Maria controlled what she conceded and carefully countered. And even though she was cleared by her boss to discount as high as 12 percent, she understood there was no need to give that much away. Not only did Maria increase her commission, but she secured better payment terms for her organization. And what did it cost her and her organization to do so? Just a portion of the discount she was authorized to give and customer access to a support line that was already in place.

But to get a good deal, Maria would have had to enter the negotiation knowing what she could concede, and then work strategically to retain and build more value in the negotiation.

> **Secret #3**: If you don't plan what you may be willing to concede, you give away more than you should.

Why You Might Not Plan for Concessions

Nothing makes the buyer's day like a salesperson who hasn't planned for concessions. It gives them the opportunity to pressure them into accepting just about any deal they lay on the table. And yet, many salespeople refuse to plan for concessions because just like identifying the worst acceptable outcome in the last chapter, they believe that if they choose what they might be willing to give away, they will end up doing so. As if knowing you can discount 12 percent means that you should give all 12 percent away.

In practice, the customer is almost always going to ask you for additional services to be included for the same price. They may even ask you to take on more risk. Or they may also ask you for a discount on items you've already offered. And if you simply agree to their demands without asking for anything in return, you are not just conceding, you are gifting them value. However, if you simply say no to each one, you may come off as unreasonable and as unwilling to negotiate. That's why smart salespeople like Maria plan what they might be willing to concede well ahead of negotiations, so they know what to do and what they could offer up as an alternative.

At the heart of a good concession strategy is one often-ignored truth: a bad deal is worse than no deal at all.

Avoid Concession Creep

Anyone in project management is familiar with the term scope creep. Scope creep happens when, after the project has started, additional deliverables are added on. For example, a wedding planner might initially agree to source flower arrangements for the wedding day and then is asked to "just throw together" bouquets for the rehearsal dinner. An additional deliverable has creeped into the scope of the project without any change to terms.

Concession creep occurs when the counterparty adds additional terms and requests, and the salesperson fails to counter. For example, a salesperson selling marketing services may agree to their standard package with payment delivered in monthly installments, only for the counterparty to ask them, over several discussions, to add additional services throughout the negotiation. If the salesperson simply agrees without countering, they've encountered concession creep.

Concession creep happens all the time in negotiations. And it isn't always as obvious as I've depicted it in the previous example. That's partly because it usually happens with an offhand comment ("By the way, can you bump up that order by a week?"), and slowly, over time. One additional service here and a deferred payment there and eventually, the deal isn't profitable.

Trendy business influencers say that giving without the expectation of getting is a powerful way to live your life. That's great in your personal and charitable life, but in B2B negotiations, that's a losing strategy. Based on insight from my procurement background, I can tell you with complete certainty that if you allow concession creep from the beginning, they will bleed you dry. It's not personal—it's their job.

To insulate yourself from concession creep, you'll need to become a master of only giving away what you might be willing to give away and always asking for something in return (this is called conditional giving, and we'll cover it later).

Concession Identification

To identify what you might be willing to give away in a negotiation, you must make a list of what you are willing to concede. You may say, "But Mark, haven't I already done that by writing down my range of acceptable outcomes for my success drivers in my success framework?" Yes, some of the work has been completed, but you may not be thinking about all the concessions you may be willing to give up.

Let's quickly review the success framework so we can uncover how concession identification fits in.

Success Framework

Success Drivers	Worst Acceptable Outcome	Target Outcome	Best Expected Outcome
Increase Prices	3%	5%	9%
Better Payment Terms	90 days	45 days	15 days
Improve Relationship	No change	Monthly Meeting	Quarterly review over dinner and monthly meeting

Figure 9

The success framework in Figure 9 is only a starting point. You now need to add any additional items that may have been left out that could be easy concessions for you to consider. Common additional items include add-ons that don't cost you or your organization much in terms of resources, like tickets to the next company mastermind, an appearance on the company podcast, access to a 24/7 customer support line, complimentary training, access to a customer library with support tools, or access to a dedicated technical account manager.

Specifically look for items that are easier for you to concede (maybe the infrastructure is already in place, like the company's support line, and the incremental cost of adding this customer to that support line is minimal) but will be perceived as a high-value item by the counterparty. (I'll teach you how to create that perception in a moment.) These are likely items that haven't been proposed by the counterparty.

Once you know what you are willing to concede, create a full and complete list. Your list might look something like this:

Prioritized Concessions
1. Mastermind tickets
2. Podcast appearance
3. 24/7 support line
4. Free training
5. Relationship Improvement Concessions (Monthly meeting)
6. Discount
7. Price concessions
8. Payment term concessions

Be mindful of how you prioritize your concessions. Remember, the best ones are perceived as high-value by the counterparty but are easy for your organization to give away.

Using Concessions to Your Advantage

You may be wondering why you should concede anything at all.

The goal of concessions is to satisfy a request from whomever is buying your stuff. But the secret to this chapter is that you do not have to satisfy the *entire* request to still make the counterparty *feel* satisfied. But to do that, you need to manage your concessions appropriately and take a layered approach to concession management.

Each layer of your concession strategy is a way to retain value, build value, and manage the expectations of the counterparty in terms of what's on the table. There are three layers of concession strategy:

1. Portional giving
2. Conditional giving
3. Managing Perceived Scarcity

You'll use all three layers in your concession strategy.

Portional Giving

The first layer of concession strategy is **portional giving**, or when you only ever give a portion of what is asked for. So if you ask me for 10 percent, I'll perhaps give you three percent. The art comes in if I can make you believe that it's really hard for me to even offer two percent. In response, you might explain that you really need at least eight. Perhaps by the end, you raise me to 4.5 percent.

Part of portional giving is a concept called tapering.

A lot of salespeople get into the habit of making their portional giving equivalent to the previous concession. This means that each time they give an increase or decrease, they do so by the same amount. For example, a two percent decrease becomes four percent, then six percent, then eight percent.

This gives the counterparty the expectation that every time they ask, they'll get a better and better deal. This is a major problem for a few reasons. First, it means that your deals aren't going to be as profitable as they should be. Second, it does nothing to create the illusion that it is difficult for you to go any lower/ higher than what you previously conceded.

To taper, you might begin at two, move to three, then 3.5, and then 3.75.

Tapering: 2 → 3 → 3.5 → 3.75

Tapering conditions the counterparty to believe that with each request, there is a series of diminishing returns available.

Conditional Giving

You may have heard of conditional giving, or the art of always asking for something in return. Every time you are asked to give something away, you're going to use the magic word "if." You'd like us to discount the service by 20 percent? That might be possible, *if* we can reduce payment terms to 30 days from 90 days. You'd like us to make a member of our team available to your team while you implement our product? That might be possible, *if* you can prepay for their services to secure them as a support role.

The key to successful conditional giving is to frame your requests in a way that doesn't come across as hostile or confrontational. The goal is to make it clear that you're not trying to be difficult or uncooperative, but rather that you're looking for a mutually beneficial agreement.

That's why the word "if" is so important in this practice. By starting your response with "if," you're essentially saying, "I'm willing to consider your request, but I need something from you in return." This allows you to make a concession without seeming weak or desperate.

Finally, be prepared to walk away if the counterparty isn't willing to meet your requests. Conditional giving only works if you're willing to stick to your guns and hold out for a mutually beneficial agreement. If the other party isn't willing to give you what you need, it may be better to cut your losses and move on to another term.

Managing Perceived Scarcity

Throughout your concession management, you must control the perception of the value of the thing you're giving away to make the customer believe it is more scarce than it actually might be.

Imagine you are looking to buy a used set of golf clubs from Craigslist. You see that a neighbor is selling some nice clubs for $250. So you walk to their house, offer to pay $200, and are then surprised that they agree right away. That doesn't feel very good, does it? Aren't you wondering why they accepted the discount so quickly? Could you have gotten the clubs for less?

Now imagine that they negotiated with you for 20 minutes. You both went back and forth, eventually buying the clubs for $230. I'm willing to bet that you would feel better about the outcome, even though it's worse than the first time around.

The seller controlled the perceived scarcity of the concession. The scarcer the item, the higher the perceived value. It's the same idea with precious gems. There's a lot of diamonds in the world, but because suppliers control how many make it to market and market them as scarce, they've made us all believe they are valuable because they are "rare." (Hate to break it to you, they aren't that scarce.)

Consider the conference tickets in the prioritization example. They may be the easiest thing to give away, but it's important to think about how you could make that item seem more valuable. Maybe you don't give away many of these tickets and could therefore say something like, "I have just one more conference ticket to give away, and we hardly ever comp these tickets. They are usually reserved for executive gifts in very large companies." Suddenly those conference tickets sound like a pretty good deal, right?

When you control the perceived value of the item you concede, you can make the counterparty feel amazing about negotiating for something that isn't hard for you to give away.

The goal is to use every layer together, in tandem. But if you've never used these strategies before, try starting with conditional giving. Even if the return isn't equal (even if you ask for something of lesser value than what you gave), it's still more than you had. And you demonstrate that you aren't someone who can be easily pushed during negotiations.

Build a Concession Road Map

Now that you understand the fundamental principles of concession strategy, it's time to build a concession road map. A concession road map serves three main purposes.

First, it helps you prioritize what you're willing to concede. The point of this exercise is to first prioritize your negotiable items. What are you willing to give away first, what would you consider giving away last, and which items won't make it onto the list at all? That way when the counterparty negotiates a really high-value item, you can offer something less valuable (to you) in return. Another aspect of prioritizing concessions is visualizing the point when the negotiation could feasibly enter the red flag zone of any negotiable item. If the counterparty negotiates past what you're willing to concede, you know you must either get the deal back on track or have a serious conversation with whomever you represent.

The second benefit of the road map is that it prompts you to map out how you will taper each item. That way, when the counterparty asks for a discount of say, 10 percent, you can find 10 percent on your road map and evaluate how far off that number is from your best-case scenario. Most high-value items, like payment terms, discounts, and contract length are easily tapered because they correspond to a number (like five percent or one year). Other items, like risk and relationships, are much more difficult to quantify. However, if you are going to map out what you are willing to concede, you must translate these items into something tangible. Of course, there are some items that you can't taper. Usually these are the lower value items that initially didn't occur to you to add to the negotiation, like a support line or free training. You likely do not need to taper these items.

The third and most important benefit of the road map is that it helps you navigate the negotiation. To understand how to use it, first review the concession road map.

Concession Road Map

Example

Success Drivers	Worst Acceptable Outcome	Move #3	Move #2	Move #1	Best Expected Outcome
Access to a Technical Account Manager	20 Hours per Month Access to a Technical Account Manager	8 Hours per Month Access to a Technical Account Manager	7 Hours per Month Access to a Technical Account Manager	5 Hours per Month Access to a Technical Account Manager	No Access to a Dedicated Technical Account Manager
24/7 Support Line	Access to 24/7 Support Line for 15 Main Contacts	Access to 24/7 Support Line for 6 Main Contacts	Access to 24/7 Support Line for 5 Main Contacts	Access to 24/7 Support Line for 3 Main Contacts	No Access to a 24/7 Support Line
Discount	-15%	-6%	-5%	-3%	0%
Payment Terms	90 days	35 days	30 days	20 days	15 days
Agreement Length	12 months	22 months	24 months	28 months	36 months
Limitation of Liability	No Cap	Capped to 130% of Annual PO value	Capped to 125% of Annual PO value	Capped to 100% of Annual PO value	Capped to 50% of Annual PO value

Figure 10

To use the road map, first locate the success driver the counterparty asked for. Based on where it sits in the road map, you can then offer a less valuable item listed above it. If the counterparty is still insistent on the higher value item, you can look at even higher value items below to counter with.

Let's look at how that might play out. Pretend I'm negotiating using the road map in Figure 10. I know the counterparty has been requesting improved service and access to experts, but they ask for a discount of 15 percent at renewal time. This is the third item on my list, but the percentage they asked for is my worst acceptable outcome for that success driver.

I need to try to protect my higher value items, so I say, "I may not be able to give you 15 percent. Earlier on, you mentioned that what was really important to you was improved availability of expert support and improved service as you move through a few difficult projects. Instead of the 15 percent discount, I may be able to give you access to a technical account manager if your company can improve our payment terms to net 15. That way, anytime you need expert advice and someone to fight for you in our business, this person will be there for you. Can you agree to that?"

In a perfect world, the counterparty would be satisfied with this exchange. But what if they aren't?

Then I keep moving through my lower value items that I think would satisfy the need they have, and I amplify the value of those things to increase the perception of value in the eyes of the counterparty. I might say, "Ok, let's scratch that. What if I can offer you access to an account manager and a 24/7 response line with improved payment terms? Can you do that?"

If that doesn't work and they truly want the discount instead of the things that would add value to their business, then I start negotiating based on the discount road map starting with Move #1. I might say, "Typically we don't do this, but given the value of this relationship, I might be able to give a three percent discount if your organization can provide us with better payment terms. Can you do that?"

Do you see how I used conditional giving, portional giving, and tapering to protect high-value items while creating the perception that the lower value items are just as good? Also, you can add in as many moves here as you deem necessary, and your concession road map will likely look different from one negotiation to the next.

It will take some practice to get comfortable with everything in this chapter. But if you start conditional giving, or only give if you get something in return, you will outperform most salespeople. Remember, never give without receiving something. Even when you're forced to give up something high-value and you can only get something small in return, it still improves the deal (and sets the precedent that you aren't in the business of gift-giving). As you get more familiar with conditional giving, start to use the full concession road map.

CHALLENGE: Build Your Concession Road Map

To build your own concession road map, start by prioritizing the success drivers you wrote down in Chapter 1. List them from easiest to most difficult to give away.

1. _____

2. _____

3. _____

4. _____

5. _____

Next, add in some concessions you may not have considered. Remember, these should be things that may be perceived as high-value by the counterparty but are financially and logistically easy for you to give away.

1. _____

2. _____

3. _____

4. _____

5. _____

Now, rewrite your concession list with the additional items prioritized from easiest to most difficult to give away.

1. _____

2. _____

3. _____

4. _____

5. _____

6. _____

7. _____

8. _____

9. _____

10. _____

Then, using your best expected and worst acceptable outcome from Chapter 2, fill in the chart in Figure 11. Remember to taper down your moves from your best expected backward.

Success Drivers	Worst Acceptable Outcome	Move #3	Move #2	Move #1	Best Expected Outcome

Figure 11

Concession road maps are valuable for several reasons. First, they help prioritize what negotiable success drivers a person is willing to concede during a negotiation. By identifying which concessions are more or less important, negotiators can offer something less valuable in return if the counterparty negotiates a really high-value item. This allows negotiators to manage their concessions and ensure they are giving away only what they are willing to concede, while also maintaining control over the negotiation.

Second, concession road maps prompt negotiators to map out how they will taper each item. Tapering means only giving a portion of what is asked for, so each time the counterparty makes a request, they get a diminishing return. Mapping out how to taper each item helps negotiators evaluate how far off a requested concession is from their best-case scenario and helps them stick to their concession plan.

Third, concession road maps help negotiators navigate the negotiation process. By having a plan in place, negotiators can feel more confident in their ability to negotiate and can ensure they are managing the negotiation effectively. Ultimately, a concession road map is a tool that helps negotiators stay in control of the negotiation and achieve their desired outcomes.

Negotiations Ninja Chapter 3 Breakdown

Secret #3: If you don't plan what you could concede, you'll give up more than you should.

- Planning your concessions is the best way to avoid over-giving.
- To identify what you might be willing to give away, make a list of concessions that are easy for your organization to give away but will be perceived as high-value items by the counterparty.
- A concession strategy should include conditional giving, portional giving, and managing perceived scarcity.
- Control the perceived value of the item you concede to make the counterparty feel good about negotiating for it.
- Build a concession road map to prioritize your negotiable items, map out how you will taper each item, and navigate the negotiation.

Now that you have a plan that includes success drivers, a range of acceptable outcomes, and a concession road map, you've done as much planning as you can without learning more information. That means it's time to switch gears.

This next phase is about the elbow grease that will make all the difference to your bottom line: research.

CHAPTER 4

REVEAL COUNTERPARTY STRENGTHS AND WEAKNESSES

A salesperson sells over $150K worth of chemicals to a manufacturing company on a five-year contract. Sounds like a good deal, right?

But the thing is, this salesperson could have added a zero to the sale. And that's exactly what a competitor did.

This salesperson met with the counterparty regularly to ask how things were going. On one such occasion, she learned that during the 2020 COVID-19 pandemic, the company had to shut down one of its two of its facilities.

"Two facilities?" questioned the salesperson, under the impression that there was only one site.

"There is now," explained the counterparty, "we had to shut down one because we couldn't get the supply we needed because of some major supply chain issues."

Armed with this new information, the salesperson did a little digging. A few Google searches revealed that supply chain issues had impeded the company's ability to procure a valuable input chemical they needed to continue operations. She estimated that the shutdown had already cost the company about $10 million in lost revenue, with the number ticking higher and higher as the weeks went on.

"We're bleeding money," the counterparty confided in her. "And there's no way of knowing when we'll be up and running again."

But the salesperson was actually familiar with this chemical. Although she had never sold it personally, she was pretty sure that the company she represented had stocked it in the past. A quick call to a colleague confirmed that her company was sitting on the exact chemical that the counterparty desperately needed to get their facility up and running.

Armed with nothing but a curious mindset, the salesperson was able to negotiate a massive, multimillion dollar contract all because she asked the right questions and found the right answers. The only person who was more excited by the deal might have been the counterparty, who now could reopen the facility. It was a fantastic deal—all because one salesperson asked a few probing questions.

> **Secret #4**: Once you understand who you are negotiating with, you have the foundation on which to persuade them.

This is why we conduct counterparty research—to reveal massive opportunities and avoid unnecessary risks.

Counterparty Research

Counterparty research is about understanding the person and the company on the other side of the negotiation. Who are they? Who do they want to be? And what is the nature of the organization they represent? Buried in those answers is information that could increase or collapse the deal. It's up to you to uncover it.

Successful salespeople need to conduct research on two levels. The first assesses the individual, or the person they are negotiating with. A strong negotiator knows who sits across from them on a surface level and at a deeper level. This includes details about who they are, but also about who they wish to be, how others view them, and how they view themselves.

The second level assesses the company they represent. The company, like the person, has a personality and culture that is essential to knowing how to approach them.

If conducting research seems like a huge investment of time, keep in mind that the amount of effort needed will change based on the risk and complexity of the deal. If you are selling to a local coffee shop with only one location, you won't need to conduct much research. But if you are negotiating a $100 million contract with an international, enterprise-level organization, you'll spend way more time learning about the organization than you will negotiating with them. Simply put, the more complex the deal, the more research it requires from you.

If you are about to enter negotiations on a large deal and you've never worked in a global sales capacity selling into various regions, the research required likely feels overwhelming. But rest assured it's well worth your time. If this sounds like you, start at the individual level and build out from there. If you know the person you'll negotiate with and you've identified the influencers, then you're well on your way to a successful deal.

Individual-Level Research

This section highlights important research questions that are outward facing (questions that you could ask others) and inward facing (self-reflective questions that you could ask yourself) that you need to answer before and/or during the negotiation.

Who am I negotiating with?

You want to know where they work, what department they work in, what they do, and what they care about. The key is to uncover motivation. If you don't know what is important to them, how can you possibly negotiate a deal that makes sense for them? And if you don't know what they want, how can you persuade them?

Once you understand their position, you can likely figure out what they care most about. For example, if the counterparty works in accounting, they likely care about budgetary control. If they work in legal, you can bet they care about risk reduction. If they work in safety, they probably care about OSHA compliance. If they work in governance, they care about data security. Are they from marketing? Then they care about lead generation and brand image. Based on their role, you can make strong assumptions about what matters most.

What are they responsible for?

Uncovering their responsibilities will further shed light on what is important to the counterparty. What work do they

deliver? What are they accountable for? What are they personally responsible for? Do they have budgetary control? At the
end of the day, every professional wants to make good on what
they've promised to deliver. If you understand what that is,
you can use that knowledge to your advantage.

Whom do they report to and what influence do they have?

It's very important to reflect on whether the person you're
negotiating with has decision-making authority and what level
of the organization they may dwell in. If the negotiation goes
off the rails, you need to locate the person to whom to escalate
the discussion. If you can no longer negotiate with the counterparty, make sure that you recognize the next person to begin
talking with.

Regardless of their position, do they have influence within
their organization? Can they strongly influence a decision? If
you were to expand into other areas, could this person help
you? Look for information that suggests whether they could be
a powerful advocate (or your biggest detractor).

Are they the decision-maker?

Ideally you should negotiate with someone who has decision-making power over your deal within the organization.
But even if you're not negotiating with someone who has
that power, try to ensure that you're speaking to someone
who has significant influence. (I call these people "major
influencers".)

This is often the biggest difference that folks see between busi-
ness-to-consumer (B2C) negotiations and B2B negotiations.

In the B2C world, it's very common to negotiate with someone who has final decision-making control, but in B2B negotiations (especially in enterprise deals) it's more likely you will speak to someone who instead has major influence over the decision that's being made and is not a decision-maker. The reality is that the person who has budgetary control over the project, contract, or the purchase of something is the one who has final say and they are likely not in the weeds of day-to-day negotiation.

The likelihood is that you're not going to be speaking directly to that person in large enterprise deals; however, you may be speaking to someone who is directly influencing or affecting the person who has budgetary control to make a decision.

No matter whom you negotiate with, you'll want to find out exactly who has the power to say "yes." Once you determine who that person is, find out whether or not you can reach them. Ask the people you've built relationships with for contact info or ask directly if that decision-maker can be made a part of the negotiation.

How do they perceive themselves?

Perception is everything in negotiation.

But it's especially important to recognize that how the counterparty perceives themselves may be different than how others perceive them.

If you're negotiating with someone young and new to the company, you might perceive them as ill-informed or even naive. But they might perceive themselves as a motivated go-getter.

Or you might think the counterparty is incredibly savvy and has a ton of leverage while they view themselves as somewhat meek and overall uncomfortable with conflict and negotiation. My point? The counterparty might view themselves differently than you do.

In most cases, it's in your best interest to treat someone how they perceive themselves. In so many ways, perception is reality. And if you treat them in a way that is counter to their self-image, you could accidentally create a bad situation for yourself. For example, if you treat the young salesperson in the last paragraph like the naive kid you think he is, he'll likely try to prove to you what a motivated go-getter he thinks he is by potentially being motivated to spend time elsewhere. Don't create unnecessary tension and conflict within the relationship because of your own perception.

How do they perceive me?

Does the counterparty view you as someone who is trustworthy, helpful, and an advisor? Or do they view you as slimy, and greasy, and manipulative—someone who would sell anything to make a buck?

Ideally, the counterparty will view you as someone who wants the best for them. If you don't currently inspire that kind of relationship, you may need to take a hard look at how you are perceived and change your approach. You need information, and the best way to get it is through ensuring that the counterparty views you as an ally and partner.

How do they perceive my organization?

Does the counterparty perceive your organization as a market leader? What might they know about your company? Are they aware of your strength relative to the competition? This question is key in evaluating how much leverage you have (or don't have) in the negotiation.

Identifying Influential Stakeholders

In nearly every circumstance, the decisions made throughout the negotiation won't be made in a vacuum. That is to say that there are likely many people involved who influence the decision. These people are **influential stakeholders**, meaning that although they aren't the decision-maker, they have a personal stake in the outcome of the deal and can therefore influence the outcome.

Influential stakeholders can appear throughout the organization. They might come from the department that will actually use the product or service, like the technicians or developers. Or they could be leaders from adjacent departments like procurement, finance, legal, safety, or data security.

Once you know who the influential stakeholders are, it's time to figure out whether they are major or minor influencers and whether they are positive or negative influencers.

Some of these stakeholders may be your biggest champions. Perhaps they have heard from colleagues that you can help them. Maybe they understand something about the industry that the C-suite doesn't, and therefore are more educated on what you can bring to the table. Maybe they've met you, and although they don't know much about what products or services you can provide, they feel that they can trust you and are excited by the opportunity.

If you decide someone is a positive influencer, then you've identified someone who could champion you throughout the negotiation process. It's important to keep that relationship healthy. This is especially important if you consider them a major influencer (someone who has direct influence over a decision). If they are a minor influencer (someone who is tangentially affected by the deal), it's best to not spend as much time developing this relationship as you would with a major influencer.

If you find negative influencers, consider how you can move them in a direction more in your favor. If that isn't possible, then your job is to neutralize dissent with overwhelming support from all the other influencers.

However optimistic the influential stakeholders may be, don't assume that everyone wants your product or service. There is no guarantee that they will want you there at all. An outside accounting service may not be warmly welcomed by a mid-level manager in accounting. A new technology developed by your company may not be loved by everyone who prefers the old way of doing things. Not everyone will be in your corner, so prepare yourself for potential pushback early.

Often, negative influencers simply don't want change to occur because change is hard. Learning new systems and adapting to new protocols or environments is stressful. Sometimes negative influencers are just annoyed that their job won't look the same after you've sold the company your solution. Take note of these influencers, as you'll want to change as many minds as possible throughout the negotiation.

Influencer Map

Pretend you sell welding services. You set out to create an influencer map to better understand who you should try to influence at a local plant to build leverage. To create this map, you'll want to begin by thinking logically about who has influence over the decision. Include anyone who has control over the project or who will use your product or service.

While examining your list, consider whether anyone doesn't want you there. Think primarily about any preexisting relationships (at a personal and professional level) with the current service provider that you may be displacing. These are your negative influencers. Next, identify whether anyone enthusiastically wants your solution. These are the people who want a change. Maybe they are unhappy with the preexisting service provider or believe there is a better way to run the operation. These are your positive influencers. You now have a list of allies and detractors.

Next, decide whether each name on the list is a major or minor influencer. An obvious major influencer is the decision-maker, as they have the power to green-light the deal. Additional major influencers might include someone who doesn't necessarily have the power to hire your services but does have a lot of respect within the organization and is majorly affected by the outcome of the deal. A minor influencer is someone whose opinion will be taken into consideration but does not have the power to single-handedly accept or reject your proposal.

Figure 12 is an example of an influencer map for welding services.

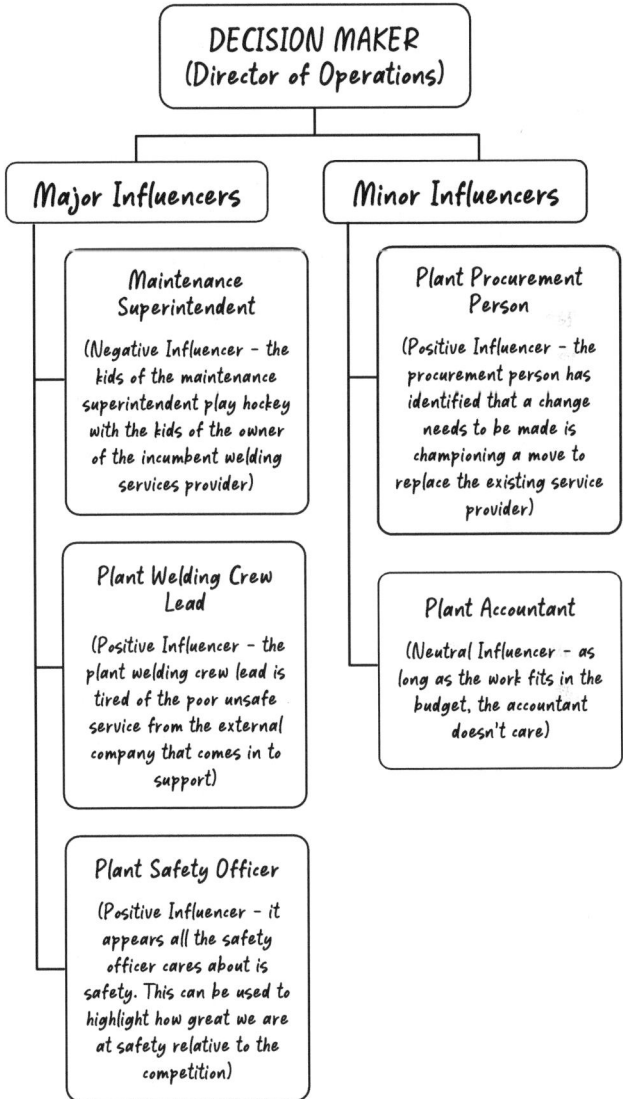

Figure 12

For many salespeople, research on the individual and stakeholder level will provide enough information to negotiate confidently. But for those selling to large organizations, research will also need to include the corporate level.

Corporate-Level Research

While writing this book, I asked one of my students what their research process looks like. They told me that they usually spend about 30 minutes online looking at the company. As I continued to probe, I grew concerned, realizing this person was negotiating big, million-dollar contracts without diving deeper than a surface-level understanding of the organization. What follows is a list of questions to ask yourself when negotiating big deals.

What is the organization that I am negotiating with?

You should be familiarizing yourself with the organization that you're negotiating with as much as you can. What industries do they operate within? What products and services do they sell? What is their relative strength and size compared to others in the industries that they sell to? Learn the terminology they use and who the competition is. You want the counterparty to feel confident that you understand their specific needs.

Understanding the industry can lead to very profitable future deals. For example, if I sell welding services and you're a large pipeline company, I know that you probably sell pipe to oil and gas, utilities, and electrical companies. In this scenario, the company sells to many industries. Understanding what those are helps you determine whether the services you provide are relevant in each vertical. If each is more or less the same, you know you have the opportunity to sell more products or services. If some are more specialized, it doesn't necessarily mean that you won't be able to sell into each vertical, but it does mean you'll likely need to tailor the conversation to a specific area.

For example, an oil and gas company might be more concerned about safety, whereas a utilities company may be more concerned about price. Of course, it's unlikely that the person you're speaking to directly has the authority to procure your product or service for every industry they sell to. But you can simply ask the counterparty if they would refer you to someone in that vertical and begin exploring opportunities from there.

What is the relative strength of the organization?

Further (and perhaps more importantly), you need to know their relative strength and size in comparison to the industry average. What is their market share? You can determine strength by looking at the number of people they employ, their revenue, and their profitability in relation to their competitors.

Determining relative strength is what I call a leverage question, meaning it will help you gauge how much leverage they have. If the counterparty has a lot of relative strength, they have much more power. If the counterparty isn't competitive in the industry, they are not entering into the negotiation with much leverage.

A major question in determining relative strength is market share. If the counterparty controls 50 percent of the market and their biggest competition only controls 15 percent, you know you are dealing with the major player in the industry. That means the counterparty controls the way that the industry moves in terms of the direction it takes, the trends it adopts, and the things it buys. When Mozilla makes a change to Firefox, it doesn't change the way people use search engines. But when Alphabet changes Google, every search engine scrambles to adapt. That's power through market share.

What do they care about?

Does corporate care about culture? Diversity? Safety? Do they preach about hard work and bootstrapping? Uncovering what the corporation cares about can help you learn how to best communicate. If they care about safety, make sure to show them how your product or service will help create a safer work environment. If corporate is all about a family at work, show them how you share those values. If you do, you'll make yourself and your product and service an easy sell, as you'll be speaking in the language of the organization.

What about regional differences?

The corporate culture might not stress safety very often, but the Dallas location that just suffered a major worksite accident probably does. Corporate could care about keeping a four-day work week, while the Montana location usually pushes for a 50-hour week. Often regional culture is different from corporate, and you should conduct research accordingly.

CHALLENGE: Conduct Research

Research is an ongoing process throughout the negotiation. If you can't answer every question right now, that's okay. Just answer what you can and resolve to find the answers to every question through further investigation or from the counterparty directly.

Individual-Level Research

Learn about the counterparty by asking yourself the following:

- What is the position or department of the person I am negotiating with?
- What are they responsible for?
- Whom do they report to?
- What is their relationship with the organization they represent?
- Are they the decision-maker?
- Are they a major or minor influencer?
- Are they a positive or a negative influencer?
- How do they perceive themselves?
- How do they perceive me?
- How do they perceive my organization?

Identify Influential Stakeholders

Write the names and positions of major and minor influencers. Once you've identified them, evaluate whether they are a positive or negative influence.

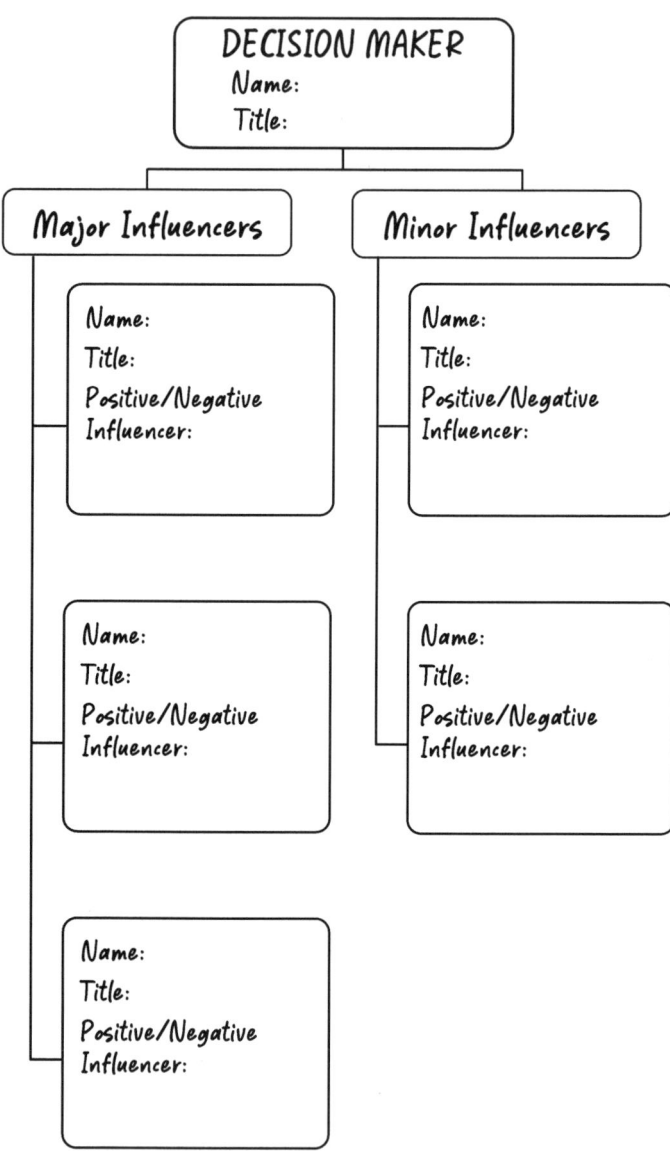

Figure 13

Corporate-Level Research

If you are selling to a large organization, make sure to include corporate-level research by asking the following:

- What is the organization that I am negotiating with?
- What is the relative strength of the organization?
- How much do they spend on the type of services I sell and where do they spend it?
- What do they care about?
- Are there regional differences?

The Final Question

After you've compiled your research, it's time to review what you've discovered through a new lens. The next question to ask is this:

Does this information create risk or opportunity for me?

For example, discovering that the counterparty has five other locations creates massive opportunities for you. Meanwhile, discovering that the head of an adjacent department has reason to resist your product or service creates risk. Systematically evaluate risk and opportunity for each question.

Negotiations Ninja Chapter 4 Breakdown

Secret #4: Once you understand whom you are negotiating with, you have the foundation on which to persuade them.

- Counterparty research is important for successful negotiations.
- Research should be conducted on two levels: the individual and the company they represent.
- The level of research required will depend on the risk and complexity of the deal.
- The more complex the deal, the more research is required.
- Starting at the individual level and building out from there is a good approach for those new to global sales.

There is a point of diminishing returns in research. If at any time you feel like the insight you gain is less than the effort you've put in, stop. That's a sign that analysis paralysis could be in your future. It is in your best interest to avoid getting so bogged down in information that you lose a clear plan forward. Stop, breathe, and recalibrate.

Lastly, remember that research is an ongoing process. You'll conduct research before and during your negotiation and may even continue to do so throughout the length of the contract. If you can't answer a question right away, you can often find that information during the negotiation process. In fact, that's precisely what we're going to do next: locate questions that create massive opportunities.

CHAPTER 5

DEVELOP QUESTIONS THAT CREATE MASSIVE OPPORTUNITIES

"I think we've got a great deal here," said Malia, a new salesperson representing a company that sells contingent labor.

They had just agreed on price, contract term, and twenty or so other items. From Malia's perspective, the contract leaned in her favor. She shook the hand of the counterparty and closed the deal.

But a month later, she received a frustrated call from her supervisor.

"Malia, the factory that you just did that 50-person contingent labor deal with just signed another deal with our competitor to bring another factory of theirs back online."

"Really?" Malia asked incredulously.

"Yes. They signed for 200 people. Were you aware that they even had another factory?"

Malia did know about that factory. The company had shut it down ages ago because of supply chain issues. Apparently those problems were sorted out.

"Well, they never mentioned it," said Malia, now a bit angry. "How could I have possibly known?"

It turns out that the reason the organization didn't tell Malia about the second facility was because they didn't believe that *any* company could provide a stable and qualified labor supply of 200 people. But Malia *did* have the labor they needed—she just didn't bother to ask whether they needed labor at any other facility. If Malia had simply asked when they were planning to open up the second facility, she could have closed the deal that was four times bigger than the last one.

> **Secret #5:** The right questions can help you uncover massive opportunities (and avoid massive risk).

This chapter reveals how to create questions to ask internally and externally in your negotiations to uncover the best possible deal.

Why We Form Questions

The questions you develop in this chapter will uncover information that may not necessarily be visible on the surface of your research. And some that aren't always available to the public. It may even generate opportunities that you never would have known about otherwise.

So many people go into negotiations completely at a loss of what to ask, thinking that the questions will magically appear in their heads exactly when they need them. They won't. Or they think they'll remember what they want to ask during negotiation, but they don't. Instead they'll end up having multiple discussions with the counterparty where fewer could have gotten the job done.

(It also makes you look like an unprepared idiot because you tend to fumble over ideas and stall until you can think of something to ask.)

That's why we're going to form questions ahead of time.

In this chapter you'll develop four sets of questions to ensure you are fully prepared to extract the information you need. The first set determines whether the counterparty can provision for *your* success drivers. The second examines and investigates the counterparty's success drivers. The third prepares you to answer the counterparty's potential questions. The fourth and final question set prepares you and your internal team for a successful negotiation.

Question set one: Provisioning for your success drivers

Question set two: Provisioning for the counterparty's success drivers

Question set three: Forecasting the counterparty's questions

Question set four: Preparing the internal team

Before we dive into each set of questions, consider delivery for a moment. How you ask these questions matters almost as much as the questions themselves. As a salesperson, it's up to you to create an environment that the counterparty feels comfortable in. Most salespeople are competent at making small talk and otherwise being friendly, and I'm confident that you know how to do that too. If you do need help on presentation, delivery, and style, look in the back of this book for a list of recommended authors. Whatever you do, do not simply read through the questions as if checking off items on a grocery list. You want to facilitate a friendly conversation, not an interrogation.

Ready? Let's begin.

Question Set One: Provisioning for Your Success Drivers

To form a question in the first set, review your success drivers from Chapter 1. Whatever your drivers are, consider what you can ask to reveal more information concerning each item.

Building Targeted, Open-Ended Questions

Each question should be **targeted** to the chosen success driver. There is no generic magic question that could lead to an opportunity—that's why we ask a set of targeted questions focused on the success driver. If they were too broad, you'd waste a lot of time getting to the level of information you need to facilitate a meaningful conversation.

The key to creating targeted questions is intention. Think clearly about what information you are trying to extract and then work backward from the ideal answer to generate the question with the highest probability of eliciting that information. Without the correct intention, you run the risk of asking vague and misplaced questions that really don't uncover much valuable information at all. That increases the amount of wasted time in a negotiation and dramatically affects the speed at which you can get to a result that you need.

When I teach question development, my students always want to know how to tell whether their questions are targeted enough.

Here's a tip: the key is to gather information about what it is you are trying to achieve during the negotiation (those success drivers). Without understanding more about what the counterparty can do with regard to those success drivers (and how they can do it), you are limiting your ability to identify areas where you can build and extract more value from the conversation.

Pretend one of your success drivers is to increase the amount of product you sell to the counterparty. Below are targeted questions that might uncover opportunity:

- What other areas of the organization may need the product?
- What inventory do they need to ensure a stable supply?
- What changes in the way we roll this out would encourage them to utilize it more?
- What are the other distribution channels and partners that could use the product or service?
- How is the company growing? (This would suggest they will need a larger volume of product.)
- What have other companies like yours done to ensure their team gets maximum value out of what they are being provided?

These questions are all targeted to uncover how you could increase the amount of product you could sell (a.k.a. the massive opportunity). There is no magic question that could lead to an opportunity—that's why we ask more than a single question.

Not only should these questions be targeted, they must also be **open-ended**.

Open-ended questions can't be answered with a simple "yes" or "no" response. These types of questions typically begin with words like "what," "how," "why," or "tell me about," and encourage the person being asked to provide more detailed and thoughtful responses.

Open-ended questions are your window into the world of the counterparty because they encourage them to provide more information about their needs, interests, and concerns. By asking open-ended questions, you can gather more detailed information about the other party's situation and better understand their motivations and decision-making process.

Part of the magic of the open-ended question is that they tend to keep the conversation flowing and encourage the other party to actively participate in the negotiation process. This can help to establish a more collaborative and productive negotiating environment where both parties feel heard and valued.

Meanwhile, closed questions are conversation killers! They produce short, "yes" or "no" answers. Have you ever been at an awkward dinner table conversation where someone keeps asking closed questions? It feels like a weird interrogation. Closed questions can stifle conversation.

They are significantly less likely to produce the treasured and helpful additional information about *what* the counterparty can provision for (in terms of your success drivers), *how* they can provision for it, and *why* they may or may not provision for it.

In fact, that's exactly how you should start your questions: with the words what, how, or why.

Here are a few examples of some targeted, open-ended questions based on our earlier example of Blue Sky Earth Moving.

Blue Sky Earth Moving: Success Drivers	Question Set One
Increase volume of services sold	What other build sites do you have and what are you doing at those sites?
	What types of equipment have you used on sites like this in the past and how many pieces were the right number for you?
	What kind of growth are you expecting?
Cross-sell additional products and services	What are the major obstacles you face on site when working with earth moving companies like us?
	What equipment do you wish you had access to for this kind of work?
	What additional help do you think you might need to make your experience as problem free as possible?
	What have companies like ours done that you love in terms of extra value provided?
	How are you planning on solving the [insert a problem that you have noticed that your company can solve that it is not currently solving] problem?
Increase the length of the contract	How long do you foresee your company needing earth moving services for this project?
	What other earth moving needs do you have after this project is finished?
	How can we work together to ensure the continued success of our partnership over a longer period of time?

Figure 14

Notice that these questions are open-ended and *extremely* targeted. Questions like "what other build sites there might be?" and "what they are doing at those build sites?" elicit a great deal of information. Ideally, you should have at least three to five questions prepared for each success driver *prior* to going into the negotiation. Do not rely on your imagination to develop these questions on the fly. Prepare them well ahead of time so that you can practice asking them.

The Power of Silence

As natural people pleasers and conversationalists, many salespeople have an awkward relationship with silence. It makes us nervous. And sometimes we react to silence by attempting to "help" the other person by answering the question for them (before they have an opportunity to answer for themselves). Or sometimes we justify the question by giving them a reason as to why we are asking the question, rather than letting them respond.

The problem is that although it may feel polite or helpful, it actually makes it less likely that you will receive an honest answer. For example, if you asked the counterparty what obstacles they may have faced during the last time that they did work like this and then justified why you were asking that question, you may be leading them to give you an answer that is related to your justification instead of the honest answer you need. Here is an example of a targeted, open-ended question asked incorrectly with justification:

Sales: "What were some of the issues you've experienced in other projects like this?"

Counterparty (thinking about the question) "…"

Sales (trying to justify their question): "The reason I ask is because I need to know whether you had issues related to [justification example]."

Counterparty (answering the question based on the justification): "Ah, no issues with [justification example]."

Justifying questions limits the potential available responses. But if you instead embrace the silence and give the counterparty time to fully consider the question, you might hear a completely different (and much more honest) answer.

Ask a question and wait for the counterparty to respond.

The first question set was all about you and your success drivers and determining whether the counterparty can provision for them. And for a lot of salespeople, this may have seemed counterintuitive, as many of us primarily think about the counterparty's needs before our own. But up next we're going to flip the script to something you're likely more comfortable with: provisioning for the counterparty's success drivers.

Question Set Two: Provisioning for The Counterparty's Success Drivers

Question set two includes questions you will ask to determine the counterparty's success drivers. As you may recall, in the first chapter we made some educated guesses about what their drivers may be. At that time we didn't know, with certainty, what those were. And assumptions without verification are very dangerous in this business. That's why we are going to vet those assumptions with question set two.

The easiest way to find out what the counterparty's success drivers are is to simply ask. Direct yet exploratory questions like, "What does success look like for you?" are perfectly acceptable.

Question Set Two: Counterparty Success Drivers

- What does a successful outcome look like to you?
- What do you want to achieve in this negotiation?
- What are your priorities in this discussion?
- What are the top three outcomes you want from this deal?
- How will you know whether you've made the right decision?
- What do you want to do with this relationship?
- How long-term do you envision this relationship?
- What are your goals for this project?
- How will you know that you've done a job well done at the end of our contract?
- What is most important to you in this deal?
- How are you rewarded/compensated?

As strange as it might sound, the counterparty might not actually know what they want out of the discussion. Asking these questions not only helps you to discover what they want but can even give them clarity, too.

How to Provision for Your Success When Focusing on Theirs

You should prepare for the event that the counterparty doesn't know how to answer questions about their success drivers. When this happens, it can seem disheartening in the moment. How are you supposed to get any information out of someone who has no clue what they want?

In fact, this is a massive opportunity for you.

When the counterparty doesn't know what they actually want out of the negotiation, it opens the door to help them envision their success with you instead of others.

Here's an example:

Sales: "What do you want to achieve from this negotiation?"

Counterparty: "…I want to…I want to ensure we get a deal that makes sense for both of us."

Sales: "Of course, so do I. And to know what makes sense for you, I need to know what you want to achieve from the negotiation."

Counterparty (struggling to determine what it is they want): "…"

Sales: "For example, many other clients like you have said that they want to reduce operational risk in the completion of the work by ensuring that whomever they contract with has industry-leading safety protocols in place because they value worker safety."

Counterparty: "Oh yes, we definitely want that."

Sales: "Fantastic. We have the best safety standards in the industry and can objectively show you how our worker safety stats exceed others in our industry. Now we know that safety is important to you and your business. But from what I recall, the timeline was also important to you. Would you say that worker safety is more or less important for you than the timeline associated with the completion of the work?"

Do you see how the salesperson showed the counterparty what success looks like with their company? When the counterparty doesn't know what they need and want, you have the chance to tell them how you fit the bill.

Now that you know the counterparty's success drivers, it's time to prepare your answers to questions the counterparty may ask you. What might the counterparty want to know from you, and how will you respond?

Question Set Three: Forecasting the Counterparty's Questions

The counterparty wants information as badly as you do. So what might they need to know?

You can likely anticipate most of the questions you will get. It is critical that you think carefully about the potential questions you may get from the counterparty and plan for them ahead of time. And while it's not an exhaustive list, here are a few you can likely count on:

- How does the pricing of your product/service compare to competitors?
- What type of support/training do you offer to clients?
- What kind of discount can you provide?
- How much faster can the work be completed?
- How can we ensure we're getting the best people?
- How does your company ensure that it can meet deadlines and deliver on promises?
- How will you customize this while maintaining cost?
- What are the risks I don't know about?
- What is the implementation process like and how long does it typically take?
- How will you measure and report on the success of the deal?

If you can answer those questions, you're off to a good start. But no matter how well you prepare question set three, you'll almost certainly get a question from left field. This exercise isn't about anticipating every single possible question from the counterparty—that's not possible. But you can predict most of their questions. And when you do get one you can't answer, it's okay to tell the counterparty that you'll follow up with the answer.

But the real challenge to this question set isn't just in antici-pating what they might ask you. It's also about preparing your answers in a way that doesn't reveal too much information about you or your organization that could reduce your lever-age. Be mindful not to disclose any information that may weaken your position. This might include bottom-line pricing, internal procedures, product or service limitations, the relative size and strength of your organization within the market that makes you sound weak, or confidential information.

While I encourage you to plan to answer strategically, I don't want you to lie. Never lie. Getting caught in a lie is one of the most self-destructive situations a salesperson can put them-selves in, as it destroys credibility.

Now that you have considered the counterparty, it's time to bring the focus back to your organization. Question set four provides a useful framework for asking important questions of oneself and the organization to ensure this understanding is achieved.

Question Set Four: Preparing the Internal Team

Question set four includes questions you need to ask of yourself and internally (within your business) to ensure you have understood the counterparty and their organization well enough to determine how to best approach the negotiation.

- Who is the decision-maker in the counterparty?
  - How can I develop a relationship with them?
  - How can I influence and persuade them to make a decision in my favor?
- Who influences the decision-maker in the counterparty?

- How can I develop a relationship with them?
- How can I influence and persuade them to make a decision in my favor?

- Who does not want this decision to be made?
  - Do they have great influence over the decision?
  - How can I influence and persuade them to make a decision in my favor?
- What could be the logical reasons that the counterparty may decide not to move ahead?
  - How can I show logic that refutes those reasons?
- What could be the logical reasons that the counterparty may decide to move ahead?
  - How can I support that logic?
- What could be the emotional reasons that the counterparty may decide not to move ahead?
  - How can I turn those emotions around?
- What could be the emotional reasons that the counterparty would decide to move ahead?
  - How can I reinforce those emotions?
- When does the counterparty need a decision made by?
  - What is the negative impact to their business if the decision isn't made by that time, and how do I amplify the pain of that?
- When does the counterparty need the solution to their problem to be in place?
  - What is the negative impact to their business if the solution isn't in place by that time, and how do I amplify the pain of that?

By answering these questions, you can gain a better understanding of the decision-making process and identify key
decision-makers and influencers. This can help in developing
relationships and in creating a persuasive approach tailored
to the counterparty's needs and concerns. Additionally, these
questions can help you anticipate and address potential objections and to identify and reinforce emotional and logical reasons for moving forward with the deal.

Building a Question Funnel

Sometimes the counterparty provides superficial responses to
our targeted, open-ended questions. These vague answers may
not fully address the intention behind our initial inquiry. In
such cases, you'll need to employ a question funnel. I'm sure
you've used a question funnel in the past, but let me refresh
your memory.

The primary goal of a question funnel is to delve deeper and
obtain more detailed information. It represents a way of struc-
turing questions rather than a step-by-step process.

For example:

Salesperson: "What challenges has your organization
faced related to this kind of work in the past?"

Counterparty: "We've struggled with working alongside
unsafe and inefficient companies. Many we've encountered in this field don't prioritize safety and efficiency like
we do."

The response, while offering some insight, doesn't provide a comprehensive understanding of the issue. The counterparty reveals that they've had difficulties with unsafe and inefficient companies, but we still lack information about why this matters to them, how they've addressed these issues, and what they expect from future collaborations.

As a skilled negotiator, you must probe deeper and encourage the counterparty to elaborate. Based on the counterparty's initial response, the example's salesperson could ask follow-up questions like:

"Where has safety most affected projects like this in the past?"

Or

"What are some of the biggest areas you've seen where efficiency was an issue?"

Or

"What were some of the things that companies were being unsafe with?"

Probing deeper helps identify potential risks or opportunities. The question funnel's objective is to uncover these risks or opportunities to inform your negotiation strategy.

Once you have enough information, ask a closed question that generates a "yes" or "no" response. For example, after determining the company's safety concerns, you could ask:

"If I could demonstrate how we can meet or exceed your expectations related to safety in the areas you shared with me, would it make sense for us to discuss the support we need from your organization regarding compensation and time to achieve these safety measures?"

By doing so, you convey your ability to mitigate their concerns while identifying an opportunity to negotiate further in your favor.

The question funnel can be summarized as follows:

1. Open-ended: begin with broad inquiries.
2. Probing: delve deeper based on the counterparty's response.
3. Closed: conclude with specific questions that require a "yes" or "no" answer.

The goal is to start with a wide-ranging question and gradually narrow down the subject until the counterparty provides specific information. When executed effectively, a question funnel can reveal hidden opportunities and insights.

CHALLENGE: Build Your Own Question Sets

In this challenge, you'll use the generic questions I've provided but tweak them to meet your specific needs. We'll start with question set one, provisioning for your success drivers.

Question Set One: Provision for your success drivers

Begin this challenge by reviewing your success drivers. Then reverse engineer them into questions.

Example

Blue Sky Earth Moving: Success Drivers	Question Set One
Increase volume of services sold	What other build sites do you have and what are you doing at those sites?
	What types of equipment have you used on sites like this in the past and how many pieces were the right number for you?
	What kind of growth are you expecting?
Cross-sell additional products and services	What are the major obstacles you face on site when working with earth moving companies like us?
	What equipment do you wish you had access to for this kind of work?
	What additional help do you think you might need to make your experience as problem free as possible?
	What have companies like ours done that you love in terms of extra value provided?
	How are you planning on solving the [insert a problem that you have noticed that your company can solve that it is not currently solving] problem?

Increase the length of the contract	How long do you foresee your company needing earth moving services for this project?
	What other earth moving needs do you have after this project is finished?
	How can we work together to ensure the continued success of our partnership over a longer period of time?

Figure 15

Now you try for each of your drivers.

Success Driver	Question

Figure 16

Now write in two additional questions for each driver.

_____

_____

_____

_____

_____

_____

_____

_____

_____

_____

If the counterparty cannot provision your success drivers, it's a red flag. Consider whether it's in the best interest of you and the organization to move forward with the negotiation. If you decide that they can provision for your success, it's time to focus on how you'll build a lasting relationship and create profitability long-term.

Question Set Two: Understanding their success drivers

Now develop the questions you will ask them to understand their success drivers:

_____

_____

_____

_____

_____

_____

_____

_____

_____

_____

_____

Question Set Three: What questions will they ask you?

Now develop the questions you think they will ask you:

_____

_____

_____

_____

_____

_____

_____

_____

_____

_____

_____

_____

Question Set Four: Self-reflection questions

Now reflect and do the work necessary to plan for question set four.

_____

_____

_____

_____

_____

_____

_____

_____

_____

_____

_____

Negotiations Ninja Chapter 5 Breakdown

Secret #5: The right questions can help you uncover massive opportunities (and avoid massive risk).

- Focus on creating questions that are specifically aimed at revealing more information about your success drivers. Intention is crucial in crafting these questions to avoid asking vague or misplaced ones that waste time and impede progress.

- Encourage the counterparty to provide more detailed and thoughtful responses by asking open-ended questions. These questions help maintain the flow of conversation and foster a collaborative negotiating environment.

- Verify your assumptions about the other party's drivers by asking direct, yet exploratory, questions. These questions can also help the counterparty gain clarity about their own goals.

- Anticipate the information the counterparty may seek and be prepared to answer common questions about your product/service, pricing, support, and potential risks. It is acceptable to admit when you cannot answer a question and follow up later with the necessary information.

- Assess your understanding of the counterparty's decision-making process, key decision-makers, and influencers. Answering these questions can help in developing relationships, creating a persuasive approach, anticipating objections, and reinforcing emotional and logical reasons for moving forward.

As we move from understanding the importance of asking targeted and open-ended questions to uncover information about both parties' success drivers, it's time to explore another essential aspect of sales: focusing on long-term relationships. Developing long-lasting connections with your clients not only ensures the sustainability of your business but also helps foster trust, loyalty, and repeat business.

In the next chapter, we will delve into the strategies and approaches that can be employed to establish and maintain fruitful long-term relationships.

CHAPTER 6

CREATE PROFITABILITY LONG-TERM

"**C**ome on, Travis," said the counterparty, "we've been doing business for years. I think we've earned an extra five percent off on this new contract."

"Fine, Ellen," responded Travis, "I'll see what I can do."

Travis was at his wits' end. He sold marketing services and worked closely with the marketing team on deliverables. He'd been working directly with Ellen for three years, and every single subsequent year was worse than the last.

It started out fine enough. Ellen had negotiated a pretty significant discount from the outset because she promised that marketing for her large organization would give them exposure. But they hadn't signed a single big contract based on their relationship with her company.

What's worse, his team would ask for information they needed, like a new brand logo or critical talking points, which she'd deliver late (if at all). It meant that no matter how early his team began work, they were chronically behind schedule, a fact which Ellen would then berate him for.

And if that wasn't bad enough, Ellen was two months late with payment. This was a big contract, and his company couldn't just float the marketing staff's salary while Ellen couldn't be bothered to sign a check. What was he going to do?

I've said it before, but I need to say it again: most salespeople are people pleasers. It's why they are so damn good at their jobs to begin with—they want to go the extra mile to make everyone happy. But it also means that they can get steam-rolled by unscrupulous people like Ellen.

If you do not set boundaries at the beginning of a relationship, all of a sudden the Ellens of the world will email you at 8:00 p.m. regularly and expect a response. They'll send late payments, and soon, you just know they'll be late every month. They ask for a discount at every meeting. At every turn they need something from you and fail to provide anything in return.

But the truth is that Travis could have built a better relationship with Ellen that would have been sustainable long-term. If he had clearly defined how they would manage work out of scope, working schedules, and late payments, it's possible that this client could have been the big opportunity that he initially thought it was.

A poor relationship is unsustainable. But a healthy one can nourish a profitable deal in perpetuity.

> **Secret #6**: It's the relationship that delivers long-term results, not necessarily the contract.

(It's not the terms of the first deal either, although that may very well set the precedent for the relationship moving forward.) Retaining and maintaining your relationships is one of the most important things you can do to increase your long-term profitability.

The Power of Long-Term Relationships

Healthy relationship building is an essential aspect of negotiations. These relationships are important because, just like in life, they can go sour. They can even be abusive.

How do I know? Because during my years in procurement, I'd take advantage of any salespeople who would give, give, give.

I'd come back to them year after year, negotiating discount after discount.

And if that sounds mean or manipulative to you, I won't argue. But I promised to tell you the truth, and the truth is that if the counterparty is any good at their job, they will always be looking for ways to make the deal more profitable for *them*. They will push you as far as you can be pushed. It's the nature of this business. And it doesn't matter how much they like you as a person. If the counterparty can make money by doing this, well, that's probably what will happen.

The parallels between personal and business relationships are infinite, and just like in a personal relationship, we teach the other party how to treat us. If you set the expectation that every time procurement asks for a discount they receive one, then that's what will continue to happen. And if you've never clearly set the expectation of what you need for a successful deal, then that's on you.

But investing in the right relationship can have the opposite effect. Remember, it's likely more lucrative for both parties to work together long-term. And it's much easier for both parties to renegotiate with someone they are in a healthy relationship with, as opposed to entering a new deal with someone else.

That's why I encourage you to invest your time and energy into building healthy, long-term business relationships.

Exactly what a positive business relationship looks like to you will be determined based on whomever you work with. One professional might want a very personal relationship, which might include having lunch a few times a year or an invitation to the Christmas party. Others might want a healthy relationship that looks like a monthly meeting and a quarterly business review. So how are you supposed to figure out what kind of relationship the counterparty wants from you?

In the last chapter I suggested that when you want information from the counterparty, simply ask for it. During the negotiation process, ask the counterparty what a good relationship between the two of you looks like. Based on the answer, you can tailor your relationship to meet their needs (and yours).

Despite the nuance of each business relationship, there are a few common factors.

A Healthy Business Relationship Is Profitable

If the counterparty views your relationship as short-term or otherwise not valuable, they won't respect it. However, a healthy, long-term relationship is one that makes money.

I've personally been forced to part ways with long-term relationships with clients who have incredible power and leverage because the relationships were simply not profitable. Often they are shocked, believing that the benefit of being associated with them was worth an unprofitable deal. But for me and the company I represented, they were just no longer worth the hassle, big name or otherwise.

You may have heard the term "sunk cost fallacy." It's the idea that we'll continue to invest in something simply because we've already invested so much into it. It's true of money (I'll continue to keep my investment in this average-performing portfolio because it already has my life savings), time (I'll keep up this ineffective workout because I've already put months of effort into it), and relationships (I'll stay with the person who isn't quite right for me because we've been together for so long and have such a long history).

Any of those sound familiar? The same is true of business relationships and contracts. "I've been with them a long time." "They've been in my account for years—"

Blah, blah, blah.

If a deal hasn't been profitable in the past and you don't see a way to make it profitable in the future, why are you wasting your time on it? Get that baggage out of your life so you can invest your time and energy into the relationships that make you money.

Of course, not all deals have to be financially profitable to be valuable. Sometimes you might not want to give up an account because it would give a competitor the opportunity to grow. Maybe you have an account that is key to an industry or geography that is critical to keep. For competitive reasons, you may decide to keep accounts that aren't as profitable as you would like.

A Healthy Business Relationship Is Respectful

Just like the salesperson in the opening story, sometimes you have to let go of profitable deals because the relationship isn't respectful.

We all know *those* clients.

They never pay on time. They don't deliver the information you need on time. They are poor communicators. They add items and expectations retroactively. They might be rude to you or your team. They treat your employees poorly.

If you consider a relationship to be disrespectful, ask yourself whether there is a price you'd accept as compensation. This is the "asshole tax," and we all know those accounts have to pay more. Sometimes double or even triple.

But some actions are so egregious—like berating your team or constantly missing payments—that you have to walk away from profitable deals because they simply aren't respectful.

Of course, as salespeople, we don't always have the ability to make that call. If you are in this situation, hopefully you've built a relationship with your senior leadership that empowers you to bring poor relationships to their attention. Explain that the client takes up five times more resources than similar portfolios. Or that they mistreat the staff. Or that they delay or miss deliverables.

You have expectations of the counterparty. But they also have expectations of you. Always be polite, courteous, and respectful. Not only is that the proper way to behave, but it has business advantages too. The only way to build long-term relationships with people is to always present yourself respectfully. As a side note, you'd be amazed at the information someone is willing to share with you if you follow this golden rule:

Be polite, courteous, and respectful.

Setting Expectations

What do you want your relationship with this person to look like?

Consider the following bullet points.

- How often do we communicate?
- What is the tone of that communication?
- How do we resolve conflict?
- How often do we meet?
- Are we both expected to be on time and prepared?

It might surprise you that it's completely acceptable—and even recommended—to directly tell someone what your expectations are for the relationship. Don't just assume that the other person will meet your needs or act a certain way. Be direct and discuss how your relationship will go.

When it comes to business relationships and relationships in general, I promote radical directness in how we treat each other. It shocks me that we expect people to know how to treat us when we haven't even bothered to tell them. Imagine if Travis from the opening story told Ellen that he doesn't work later than 5:00 p.m. and won't respond to emails past that time. Or if he created a new contract when additional items were added. It would have completely changed the nature of their relationship for the better.

Become a Member of the Team

During negotiations, it can feel like you and the counterparty are on totally different teams. And at this point, you kind of are. But ultimately you and the counterparty will work toward a common goal, and that makes you teammates.

At the end of the day, we both have the same objective: to ensure the customer has everything that they need to be able to do the things that they need to do. So as long as we're working toward that objective together, we are going to have a great working relationship.

Prepare for Disagreements

In Chapter 9 I'll walk you through strategies to deploy if and when the counterparty becomes angry. But it's important to use similar strategies throughout your relationship. So what happens if and when you disagree?

Set the expectation that if tempers ever rise, you'll reconvene at a later date or later in the day. It's important to let people cool off and ask them to return with a list of their concerns. Then you can work through them together, as a team.

Further, make sure the counterparty understands that you will always hear out their concerns. When they do share them, keep your mouth shut until they finish speaking. There will be a time for you to respond, but be respectful and let them finish. Approach the discussion from the perspective that you can and will find a resolution.

CHALLENGE: Reflect on Your Relationships

This challenge is designed to evaluate the strength of your business relationships.

First, make a list of all your current most important business relationships, including clients, vendors, and partners. Write the relationship you are most uncertain about in Figure 16. Then for each question provided on the left column, write your answer in the right.

Company Name:	
Is it a healthy and profitable relationship, or is it not worth the hassle?	
Could it be more profitable? How?	
Does this company treat you and your team with respect?	
Have they done anything disrespectful in the last three months?	
If so, did you respond by setting a boundary? If not, write down a boundary you could create to salvage your relationship.	
How often do you communicate?	
How often do you meet?	
How do you handle conflict?	
Have you made your expectations clear?	

Figure 17

Once you complete this challenge for one relationship, continue the process and evaluate all of your working relationships. Remember that you and the counterparty are ultimately working toward a common goal. Approach disagreements with the expectation that you can find a resolution.

Finally, ask yourself if you're investing enough time and energy into building healthy, long-term business relationships. Remember that these relationships are essential to successful negotiations and can be more profitable for both parties in the long run.

Negotiation Ninja Chapter 6 Breakdown:

Secret #6: It's the relationship that delivers long-term results, not necessarily the contract.

- Healthy, long-term relationships in sales are crucial. Prioritize building strong connections that benefit both parties, as they tend to be more lucrative and easier to renegotiate.

- Tailor your approach to each business relationship. Ask your counterpart what a good relationship looks like to them and adjust your interactions to suit both of your needs.

- Evaluate whether deals are financially viable and worth the time and effort invested. Consider cutting ties with unprofitable deals to focus on those that bring value.

- Respect is a cornerstone of healthy business relationships. Be polite, courteous, and respectful to your counterparts and expect the same in return. Walk away from profitable deals if the relationship is disrespectful and harms your team.
- Promote radical directness in setting expectations for your relationships, be prepared to handle disagreements respectfully, and work toward common goals as a team.

As we've explored the importance of cultivating healthy, long-term business relationships, it's clear that the foundation of any successful partnership lies in effective communication and mutual understanding. However, there comes a time when you need to influence and persuade your counterparts to see things from your perspective, to make decisions that align with your goals, or to simply drive a deal to a successful close.

In the next chapter, we will delve into the art of influence and persuasion, equipping you with powerful techniques and strategies that will not only strengthen your existing relationships but also help you achieve your objectives in negotiations and everyday interactions.

CHAPTER 7

BUILD INFLUENCE AND PERSUASION

"**Y**ou see, Clay, my software is one of the safest options for growing businesses like yours. In fact, this is why companies focused on steady, predictable outcomes choose us." Len was hoping to persuade Clay to choose an innovative software. The company was relatively new, and so Len figured that he'd talk about what a safe option it was.

Len felt like the meeting went great and was ultimately surprised when the company went in a different direction. What gives?

It turns out that if Len had focused more on the newness or the innovative aspects of the product, he would have had a better chance of influencing Clay. Clay wanted to be an innovator and establish his company at the forefront of their niche. By playing up what a safe choice the software was, Len put the nail in his own coffin.

Not everyone wants to play it safe. But not everyone wants to make waves, either. That's why great salespeople are flexible in how they talk about their products and services so that they can speak in the language the counterparty wants to hear. If you can learn that language, you can become a great negotiator.

Secret #7: Anyone can learn to be more persuasive, they just need to speak the right language.

The Language of Persuasion

In a romantic relationship, if you want the other person to do more chores, the last thing you want to do is nag them about it. "Why don't you ever shovel the sidewalk?" or "Put your dishes away!" rarely produce the desired result.

In a healthy relationship, you might persuade your partner to change their behavior by first complimenting what they do well. After a conversation about the behaviors you generally appreciate—like how they always start the laundry or keep the windows clean—your partner is much more receptive to feedback. Then you can politely say something like, "I really love how you always load the dishwasher, it's amazing. Could you also help me by cleaning up the counter space after dinner? Would you help me with that?" And of course your partner responds, feeling appreciated, "Of course!"

By definition, persuasion is the act of influencing someone to do something that they didn't originally intend to do or to believe in something that they didn't originally believe in.

But persuasion and influence are not synonymous with manipulation. Rather, it's really about encouraging someone to behave in a way that better facilitates a healthy, long-term relationship, not bending them to your will. And the same is true of business relationships.

Persuasion can take many forms. You might persuade someone through body language, words and tone, logic or emotion, or strategic timing. One of my buddies recently bought a TV stand. It wasn't a cheap IKEA stand—it was a beautiful, hand-crafted piece of solid-wood of furniture. He couldn't take it with him in a move, so I offered to buy it from him for $500. But he decided he was going to try to move cross country with the thing and declined my offer. No problem.

But as he transferred, sold, or gave away more and more of his stuff, this TV stand remained. Eventually, he realized that the stand was just too big of a pain to move. "How about I sell it to you for $500?" he asked me.

I grinned at him and said, "I don't know, it looks pretty heavy. I'll give you $100." He rolled his eyes but accepted the offer. The thing is that sometimes persuasion is about waiting for the circumstances to tilt in your favor. As far as the TV stand goes, I just had to wait until it was such a pain for him that he was willing to accept a low offer just to get it off his plate.

We'll start with step one, identification.

Step One: Identify

You'll begin this process by identifying who needs to be persuaded. Looking at your influencer map, who has the power to say "yes" and influence "yes"? The key here is to focus on the major influencers and not the minor influencers.

There are three steps to use to persuade the counterparty. The first is to identify who must be persuaded, which you'll do with the help of your influencer map. Next you'll identify what they need to be persuaded of. While that may seem obvious, you'd be surprised how many people try to be persuasive without actually knowing what change in behavior they'd like to see.

Finally, you'll identify their current position in relation to what you want them to do. How far away are they from doing what it is you want? A devout practicing Catholic won't easily (or ever) be persuaded to become an atheist, while an agnostic might become one with the help of a well-timed, logical argument and a glass of whisky.

It doesn't take much persuasion for a firefighter to hose down a burning building. Or a parent with children inside to help them to safety. But a stranger off the street? There is little incentive for them to put themselves in harm's way. While maybe a bit crude, these examples highlight how different people need more or less persuasion to take a specific action or adopt a certain belief.

It also highlights another very important point about ability. A firefighter, for example, is very capable of performing their job (fighting fires), whereas an unprepared person walking by a fire not only lacks incentive, but they probably couldn't be very effective even if they wanted to be. If the person you are trying to persuade can't actually perform or strongly influence (a minor influencer) the act you need completed, then your efforts are likely being wasted. That means that you'll need to identify and persuade someone capable of producing the result you want.

Step Two: Get Their Attention

In negotiations, it's pretty common that the person who you need to persuade isn't paying you any attention at all. This is a big problem, considering that no matter how you choose to persuade someone, you can't do it if they are not paying attention to you.

Now, are you going to be able to 100 percent get their attention all the time? No, of course not. But you do have to think of ways to improve the probability of success. And there are two things you can do to get someone's attention to persuade them, that in my experience, deliver amazing results.

The first is to display examples of where you have been successful at helping people, just like those folks you are trying to persuade, be successful at achieving their goals. The human resources director who is hesitant to sign off on your consulting deal for the organization might be more open to it and you may get their attention faster if you can show how it has been successful in other organizations with folks just like them.

The next is to play the part. Successful people dress well for their audience. They are well groomed. They have clean, white teeth and good posture. They smell good. They walk into a room with a confidence that suggests to the world that they know you want their product, you just don't know what it is yet. All that while maintaining an air of approachability.

I have a very good friend who (when we were young) dyed his hair slightly gray so that he would be taken more seriously by senior executives. Many attractive people wear glasses to look more approachable. We naturally present ourselves differently for work than for a night out. Examine how you currently present yourself to the world and consider what it might mean for your career to play a new part.

In a culture focused on being "authentically you," it's totally unpopular to suggest that a person should dress and act a certain way to persuade others. I've had to change myself *substantially* over the years to become more persuasive. From how I talk, to how I look, to how I conduct myself socially. It all had to change. To be the person I want to be, I've had to work on myself consistently over time.

I once heard a friend tell another friend who was seriously obese that they were perfect just the way they were. And you know what? I thought it was terrible advice then, and I still think it's bullshit. No matter how great you are, you can improve. And the flip side is that no matter how big the job of self-improvement seems, the good news is that change is totally possible. People change for the better every day.

Instead of telling people they are perfect the way they are, I think we should all remind each other that we all suck (at least a little bit). There is always room to improve.

A lot of people are going to give me flack for saying this, but come on, let's be honest with each other; maybe the "authentic" you sucks. Maybe who you are right now is perceived as lazy and gross. No one will be persuaded by that person! To be clear, I'm not saying that you shouldn't express parts of who you are. But let's make sure you play up your positive attributes and do your best to lessen your worst.

I know a few readers are offended right now. And many of you are probably thinking, *People shouldn't have to do this! They should just be who they are, and people should accept them for who they are! Surely we aren't so judgmental in this day and age, right?* But the thing is, we *are.* And I promised to help you make more money, even if that means you don't always like what I say.

The truth is that how you present yourself to the world matters, *especially* if you're a salesperson. You don't have to change everything about you. But you do have to take a self-inventory and work on what you have the power to improve. I'm not a 6'3" blonde dude with huge muscles and a stunning jawline. So I have to change the way I present myself to be able to compete at that level, because otherwise I'm going to lose out.

To level the playing field, I have to focus on my strengths and fortify my weaknesses.

Tailor your clothes. Diet and exercise. Focus on your voice and delivery. Walk with good posture. Develop some great stories and interesting anecdotes. Pay attention to how you speak, too. As much as it sucks, in my experience, a lower voice generally means people will take you more seriously (unless it's comically low). Too fast of a pace can make you appear more anxious and higher strung, too slow can make you sound unintelligent. Too loud can be obnoxious, too soft can be annoying. Try to adjust your accent, tone, pitch, and pace to the region that you are negotiating in.

Do all these things and you might find that you command much more attention in your work life (and personal, too).

Step Three: Condition the Counterparty

In the beginning of this book, I told you a story of a time when I was in procurement. In the story, I seeded the idea that the counterparty was a collaborative person. Throughout that dinner and during the formal negotiations, I continued to remind him of what a collaborative person he was. This made him much more willing to be helpful, and that ultimately led to him giving me exactly what I wanted.

I was essentially conditioning the counterparty over time to get him to behave in a certain way or believe a certain thing by focusing his attention on it. Now, you can't turn a Democrat into a Republican through conditioning, but you can bring out traits they already possess that work in your favor.

Here are a few common labels that may help:

- Collaborative
- Hardworking
- Teammate
- Easygoing
- Rational or intelligent
- Open
- Flexible
- Great at building relationships

Over time, you can condition the counterparty to take on these traits when they work with you. The more flexible, collaborative, or open the counterparty, the more likely they are to agree to your terms.

The Four Layers of Persuasion

With some of the basics of persuasion out of the way, we can focus on how to structure a persuasive argument. According to Aristotle in his work on rhetoric, there are four levels of persuasion: logos, pathos, ethos, and kairos.

Logos

The first layer of persuasion is logos, or logic. During logos based, persuasive arguments, you'll present the counterparty with a logical reason to behave a certain way or believe a certain thing.

If you want your partner to pick up around the house more, a logical argument might stress how it would improve your relationship or why it would make their morning routine more efficient. If you're a salesperson in data security, the logical argument for the chief information officer (CIO) might be that if they sign on to your service, they will be more secure. If you're the same salesperson but the counterparty is the head of finance, your logical argument might be that if they sign on to your service, they'll ensure that their budget is going to be utilized efficiently and effectively.

Notice that the logical argument is tailored to your audience (a.k.a. the counterparty). Your logical reason for them to take a specific action, like purchasing your warranty, is going to change based on whomever you are speaking to.

But what if you are speaking to someone who influences the decision but doesn't have the power to sign the contract? In that case, simply ask the person who they report to or who they will tell about your product and service. Find out where they work and what their relationship is to whomever you are talking to. Once you know that, you can give them specific logos-based, persuasive arguments that you think the other person will care about.

Pretend I'm selling a marketing package to a company. I need to make a logos-based argument to the influencer that is attractive to them *and* the decision-maker. Currently I'm talking to Louise. She won't be signing the contract, as she is the head of the in-house marketing team. However, she seems to have a very close relationship with the CEO, who will ultimately make the decision on whether to purchase services.

"Louise," I might say, "I can't wait to provide your stellar team access to our large resource base. Together, I'm certain we are going to make a campaign you're really proud of. Not to mention that I'm sure Jane (the CEO) will be excited about our reach. We've helped boost great teams like yours by giving them the tools to speak directly with more customers, often increasing reach from a local level to a regional one, which can increase exposure tenfold."

Notice how I provided Louise with the logos-based argument that she'll have greater resources at her fingertips but also included the logos argument that she can repeat to Jane that the company will increase reach by 10 times? It's a good idea to feed influencers logical arguments that they can elevate to decision-makers, especially if you currently do not have direct access to them.

If this feels weird at first, consider how easy you are making their job. You've given them a paint-by-numbers solution to whatever issue your product or service will fix. And when the company you proudly represent knocks it out of the park, the influencers in your corner will have been a part of that solution.

While I gave this example for logos, it works for all areas of persuasion, including the next: pathos.

Pathos

I discussed logos first because it's often the most familiar to people. But the most important level of persuasion on this list is pathos, or emotion. Many folks argue, and I agree, that people make a decision first on emotion, and then retroactively justify it to themselves and others with logos. You buy that car because it makes you feel wealthy, and later justify it with logic by saying you made the purchase because of the resale value. In this way, pathos and logos work together. But for this layer, you must ask yourself, "What would emotionally compel someone to make a decision in my favor?"

First, consider where the counterparty is emotionally with respect to deal. If they feel great about it, then your job from here on out is to simply deliver what you promised and manage that relationship. But if they currently do not want to move forward with you, then you must understand on an emotional level why they feel that way. Are they scared of change? Does your product or service threaten their current position? Do they dislike you personally? Have they been burned before? Do they not trust you? After you brainstorm how they may be feeling, it's time to try to change it.

To change an emotion, you need to make the other person *feel* secure. To do that, you must first label their emotion. Are they upset? Nervous? Wary? I might say, "I know we've had a discussion about how this could help you, and even though there appears to be a good business case to adopt my service, it feels like you might be feeling frustrated about this." Then I pause and wait for a response. Ideally, if I have labeled their emotion correctly, they will confirm what I have labeled.

If I didn't label it correctly, they will most likely correct me. They might say, "It's not so much that I am frustrated, it's that I'm bothered by…" This is ideal. If you understand how they feel, you can work to address that feeling in a positive way. Label their emotion, talk about it, and learn why they feel the way they do.

The counterparty may very well feel afraid, or angry, or any kind of strong emotion. But when you label it, aim for softer language, like the labels that follow.

Common Pathos Labels

- Uncertain
- Nervous
- Apprehensive
- Agnostic
- Unprepared
- Unsure
- Frustrated
- Bothered

You can also try to guide them through their feelings by taking them through the journey of another customer. I might say, "When we ran this project with Bill at his company, Bill also felt bothered. He thought that it was a big investment, and to be frank, Bill thought, 'That's a lot of work to get this return.' And he actually felt very worried about it. And you know, what we did with Bill...," and talk them through a specific plan of action.

In my experience, people often try to avoid feeling negative emotions or making decisions that could lead to painful experiences. So, we need to guide them through the process of how we can help them overcome or avoid those negative emotions.

Within a business context, here are some of the things people are most fearful of:

- Potential for career risk
- Volume of work needed to implement
- Management required
- The fear of making the wrong decision
- The cost associated with the decision
- The return on investment

So I might say, "What Bill found was that if he continued along in this direction, these painful things happened," and then I would describe those things. They could include financial stress or professional embarrassment—anything painful. But then I'd show them how I helped guide Bill from that painful situation into a pleasurable one. Maybe I helped Bill make a heap of money or impress his boss. Whatever the story, make sure to guide the counterparty to the end they desire.

At the end of the day, a pathos argument is about labeling the negative emotion they are currently feeling and then mindfully leading them to a positive one. Show them how, if they agree to your terms, you will make them more money, impress their boss, and bolster their career. That's what we all want, right? Show them that working with you means success.

Ethos

Ethos means demonstrating your credibility. Why should the counterparty believe you? Why should they trust you? What qualifies you and your organization to deliver a solution?

Ethos includes the following:

- Knowledge
  - o How much do you know about their industry and their specific wants and needs?
- Skills
  - o What skills do you possess that will allow them to achieve their goals?
- Ability
  - o Do you and your organization have the ability and capability to deliver on what you promise?
- Authority
  - o Can you speak confidently about their industry?
- Education
  - o Do you have the pedigree and intelligence to serve their needs?
- Experience
  - o Are you experienced in this area?
- Certifications
  - o Do you have any proof of efficacy?

- Social proof
  - Do other organizations recommend you?

But it's not just about having everything listed above.

It's about presenting that information the right way.

Simply put, you don't want to come across as an egotistical jerk.

It takes delicacy to spread this information out throughout a conversation. You want to make sure that the counterparty understands that you are credible, but you also don't want to be self-aggrandizing. To establish credibility, you might say something like,

"As someone who's been through this before, here's what's likely going to happen next..."

Tell stories about organizations like the counterparties that you've helped before. Show them that you've delivered on a similar project. And demonstrate your knowledge of the industry.

Now that you've created an argument based on logos, pathos, and ethos, it's time to add in the final layer: kairos.

Kairos

Kairos is timing. Remember my friend with the cool TV stand? The reason I bought the stand for $100 instead of $500 is because I waited for the right timing.

How has the market changed since you last spoke to the counterparty? What changes on the horizon might make the deal more or less profitable for you in the future?

Consider how current trends, like inflation, the price of money, and political issues impact your industry.

Of course, in the fast B2B world, we don't always have the luxury of waiting for the perfect moment to enter negotiations.

However, kairos isn't just about choosing the right time to enter negotiations. It's also about choosing the right time to ask a sensitive question or choosing to make small talk before entering a difficult negotiation. Keep in mind that there is always a right and wrong time to ask specific questions.

Further, there is a right and wrong time to negotiate. The worst time to schedule a negotiation is for a Friday afternoon. It's just common sense, right? Unless you want the counterparty to make rash decisions and hurry the discussion (which is possible), don't try to have a difficult conversation right before the weekend.

Timing matters—use it to your advantage.

CHALLENGE: Run a Persuasion Diagnostic

How persuasive are you? This challenge is about self-reflection. And to do it, you certainly need thick skin and possibly a stiff drink. But I wouldn't ask you if it wasn't worth your time.

While writing this book, I asked myself, "Would you want to buy from me?" When reviewing my website, I decided "no" and completely redid the entire thing. There wasn't anything technically wrong with the Negotiations Ninja's website, it just didn't feel right. Many years ago I asked a similar question and started to hit the gym after. Self-reflection is difficult and sometimes painful, but we are always better for it.

A surgeon who wouldn't perform their own surgeries or a writer who wouldn't write their content is in trouble. So too is a salesperson who wouldn't buy from themselves. To improve, you'll need to take a hard look in the mirror.

In the following table, you'll see two columns. The first column asks you to describe what other people see when they look at you. Try to be objective and honest. The second column asks you to describe how you would like to look to others. Include specifics like "I'm wearing a nice suit," but also feelings like "I am in control." Use the space below each prompt to write.

How does my appearance look to others?	How do I want to look?
How do I sound? (Record yourself)	Would I want to speak like me? How do I want to sound?

How do I make people feel when I enter a room?	How do I want to make them feel?
Am I approachable?	What would make me more approachable?
Am I professional?	What would make me appear more professional?

Persuasion Strategy

Think about the next negotiation you go into and whom you need to persuade. Then, ask the following questions. Write your response in the space below.

_____

_____

_____

What could the logical reasons be why that person should change their mind?

_____

_____

_____

What could the emotional reasons be why that person should change their mind?

_____

_____

_____

How can I layer my credibility into the discussion?

_____

_____

_____

What can I do to increase my perceived credibility?

_____

_____

_____

Negotiations Ninja Chapter 7 Breakdown:

Secret #7: Anyone can learn to be more persuasive; they just need to speak the right language.

- Logos: Craft logical arguments tailored to your audience, focusing on rational reasons for them to adopt a specific behavior or belief. Understand their needs and present a solution that aligns with their goals.

- Pathos: Appeal to emotions by identifying and addressing any negative feelings your counterparty may have. Guide them from their current emotional state to a more positive one by demonstrating how your proposal will benefit them.

- Ethos: Establish your credibility by showcasing your knowledge, skills, abilities, and experience. Present this information delicately throughout the conversation to avoid coming across as arrogant, and use stories or examples to demonstrate your expertise.

- Kairos: Be mindful of timing when negotiating or making your argument. Consider external factors, such as market changes and trends, as well as internal factors like scheduling meetings at optimal times, and asking sensitive questions at the right moments.

At this point, you are in a strong position to begin negotiating. You have a success framework, multiple question sets, and the foundation to increase your persuasiveness. But you still aren't quite ready to negotiate. This next chapter uncovers what you need to understand to prepare for your next negotiation.

CHAPTER 8

PREPARE FOR NEGOTIATIONS

I was in the thick of a negotiation for contract labor worth tens of millions of dollars. We'd been negotiating for months and were effectively stuck in the weeds. By the end, I was fighting fiercely for terms that I thought were important. But after months without any progress, I finally asked for support from my boss.

I explained where we were and why the counterparty just wouldn't budge on adding a few more tools to the various on-site toolboxes.

She listened quietly, and then asked, "Wait, what exactly do you want included?" I explained that I was worried that the counterparty wasn't going to provision the workers with the right tools.

"I think you need to revisit the goal here, Mark," she said. "What exactly do you want to accomplish here?"

"I want to make sure that the counterparty can fulfill what we agreed on," I responded. "We just disagree about what equipment should be onsite to do that."

"Then add a line that the toolboxes will be equipped with the appropriate equipment for the job," she suggested.

That's when I realized I had wasted the last three months negotiating a term that ultimately, they didn't care about. Meanwhile, an entire build site was on hold, waiting for the contract to be signed. The counterparty and I were so focused on small items that by the end, neither of us were keeping in mind the ultimate goal of the negotiation.

If you are new to negotiations, you might be imagining your first deal as a solitary pursuit. In fact, team-based negotiations almost always produce better results. Luckily, I had someone to reach out to for support. But if I had worked with the right team from the beginning, this never would have happened.

Secret #8: The key to avoiding massive screwups is to work with a team.

If you negotiate on your own, you will miss something. It's inevitable. You'll fail to notice a look between the counterparty representatives when you bring up the timeline. Or the change in the counterparty's voice when they broach the topic of payment terms. Or you'll mishear an important date, fail to write it down, and begin your relationship at a disadvantage.

In this chapter you'll learn about four critical roles that must be filled during a negotiation. If you don't have the luxury of a team, that means you'll fill every single role. And as you likely know from other areas of life, when you perform too many responsibilities, something inevitably falls through the cracks. You can't hear every single word while simultaneously documenting exactly what was said. And you can't observe the counterparty while taking notes. And you can't lead the discussion while keeping track of critical dates.

If it's possible to have a team, use one.

Often, the reason people don't have teams is primarily a result of budget. Maybe your organization just can't commit that many people to a single negotiation. For any of the leaders that might be reading this, it's up to you to decide at what risk level or at what revenue level you're willing to throw a team at something. In my experience, you generally just get better results if you have a team-based approach.

So let's uncover why and how teams are so powerful.

The Team Structure

There are four critical roles in a team: the negotiator, project manager, observer, and advisor. We'll start with the role that you—the reader—will most likely play.

The Negotiator

A negotiator has a lot of responsibilities. They introduce the team at the beginning of the negotiation, lay out expectations, set the agenda, ask the questions, and guide the conversation. This means that they also set the tone for the negotiation. A calm and strong presence sets the stage for an effective and efficient conversation.

Most of this book has been dedicated to the role of the negotiator. A negotiator uncovers success drivers, builds a range of acceptable outcomes, conducts concession planning, leads counterparty research, and builds question sets. They then use those tools to lead the discussion. Considering the real estate already dedicated to this role, I won't spend much time fleshing it out here.

But I do want to provide a warning.

Many salespeople make the mistake of viewing the negotiator as the most important role on the team. But there is a danger in believing this, which I'll address shortly. Just because the negotiator is the primary subject in this book does not make them the MVP. In fact, there is another member who is truly the unsung hero of team-based negotiation: the project manager.

The Negotiator

- Does most of the talking
- Asks questions
- Guides the discussion
- Controls the negotiation

The Project Manager

Don't confuse the project manager with a scribe—the project manager is so much more than a notetaker.

Not only do they take the notes that you'll build your negotiation off of, but they also create summaries and records of what was agreed upon, what was left for another time, who is responsible for deliverables, and what important dates and numbers were discussed. What they choose to record and how they record it becomes the skeleton of the project.

Encourage your project manager to use a RACI chart or something similar to keep the negotiation moving forward and to keep communication flowing and managed well within the team.

A critical aspect of the project manager role is to follow up with the people responsible for each deliverable. So if someone is responsible for finding out whether the timeline on a deliverable is still going to be met, the project manager follows up with them. This kind of accountability and follow-through ensures that the negotiation doesn't languish. So many negotiations drag on and on solely because there isn't anyone to follow up with each party to ensure they are finishing their tasks.

Another critical role of the project manager is to compile everything agreed on into a contract that makes sense. The single biggest problem that I see with most contracts is a poorly written or incomplete scope of work. And a big reason why that's not done well is because no one is taking good, accurate notes during the discussion. Then inevitably, six months to a year later, one of the parties says something like, "Hey, we need to get paid for this."

To which the other party responds, "I don't know what you're talking about—it's not in the contract."

"But we talked about it."

"I don't remember that."

Too bad, I guess. Our memories suck. I don't know about you, but I don't recall what I had for dinner two nights ago, let alone terms that were agreed to on one of 10 negotiation talks that took place a year ago. Unless agreements are documented, they may as well have not been discussed at all because someone is going to forget about or misremember them (or at least say they did).

Not only does the project manager create summaries for both parties, but they make internal notes as well. They can document any areas of opportunity or weakness noticed by the team to be discussed at the debriefing. They can also note successes and failures, areas of improvement, and the mood/tone of the counterparty. These notes can be invaluable as the negotiation takes place.

Lastly, the project manager gets written confirmation by the counterparty on what was agreed to. I often ask my project manager to create a negotiations summary at the end of each meeting. The team reviews the summary, removes any notes that should be kept internal, and then the project manager sends the summary to the counterparty. At the end of the email, they write something like this:

"If the above terms aren't adjusted by your team by MM/DD, we will collectively agree that they are accurate and move forward with next steps."

This summary and proof of agreement moves the negotiation forward, documents in writing what was agreed to, corrects any incorrect assumptions made by either party, and keeps everyone honest about what was said. As you can see, the skill of the project manager will directly be reflected in the strength of the contract.

The Project Manager

- Takes internal notes
- Follows up on tasks to complete
- Builds internal summary
- Creates external summary
- Provides written records

With the project manager frantically making notes and the negotiator leading the discussion, there is no one left to observe what is happening on a macro level. That's why you'll also need an observer.

The Observer

The observer watches how everyone behaves and listens to what they say. They notice how someone changed the intonation of their voice when a particular subject was discussed and how someone responded physically when asked a certain question. While everyone is busy, the observer is vigilant, noticing body language, pitch, pace, tone, and volume. They notice when the counterparty gives a roundabout answer and how quickly they provide responses.

They may take a few notes (remember that memories suck) but mostly they are watching and listening, making sure the team doesn't miss the high-level flow of information while they are focused on nuance and detail.

The observer, in my opinion, is a luxury role. You don't *have* to have it. But it's really nice to have. If you can't spare another person to act as the observer, you can use a recording device instead (get permission to do this before you record anything). Just remember that you may miss out on some details.

> The Observer
>
> - Notices high-level trends and flows
> - Watches and listens to the counterparty
> - Catches anything missed by the other team members

Now that the negotiator, project manager, and observer are all in the room, your team needs someone on the outside to offer support and guidance.

The Advisor

Every team needs a good advisor. This is someone who isn't necessarily present at the negotiation but is always a phone call away when the team gets stuck, needs support, or wants to discuss strategy. They are generally in a supervisory role and have been around awhile. They have experience and know the business. It could be someone like the vice president or head of sales, but can be anyone who has the ability to zoom out and observe the negotiation from afar.

Don't think you need an advisor?

Maybe not—but you probably do. So many negotiators want to be the hero and let their ego get the best of them. In the opening story, I told you about how I nearly ruined a negotiation because I didn't want any outside help. Don't beat your head against the wall while wasting resources.

The Advisor

- Offers support when the team needs help
- Guides team members
- Aids with strategy
- Has a birds-eye view
- Is experienced and knowledgeable

Hopefully I've been able to persuade you to use a team whenever you're able. As I've said, team-based negotiations generally produce the best results. But that doesn't mean that there aren't some issues that can pop up when working closely with colleagues.

What Can Go Wrong With a Team?

Having a team is great, but only if the team understands what they are supposed to do. If you enter a negotiation as a team but no one really understands what their roles and responsibilities are, then everyone's going to talk over each other. Some people will contradict others. And still others will say things that they shouldn't. And once the counterparty notices that there may be contradiction or conflict between two or more team members, a good negotiator will create a rift between those two and promote infighting, effectively distracting the team from the overall purpose of the negotiation.

If I were negotiating with a team and two members contradicted each other, I would immediately identify that as an opportunity to wedge myself in between by supporting one person. I'd make that team member feel supported and in control, which would gain me favor with them. All of a sudden, I'm allied with a member of the counterparty, which makes it much easier to get what I want from them.

So how do you prevent fissures in the team?

Create Complete Equality

If there isn't complete equality on a negotiation team, there is a danger of someone who has a more senior role within the team railroading everyone else and going rogue. Or there's a danger that the person who is designated as the negotiator will take over that negotiation. Unless there is total equality, there may as well not be a team at all.

Equality manifests as the ability for anyone on the team to call a time-out.

That means that when someone (usually the negotiator, as they are the ones talking) makes a mistake, says something incorrect, or says something they shouldn't have, the project manager or the observer can and should call a time-out, which everyone respects. The team can then take as much time as they need—five minutes, two hours, two days—to get back in sync.

Imagine you're in a team negotiation with some jerk named Jerry who's got 35 years of experience. Unfortunately, Jerry has been making unnecessary concessions in all of their negotiations for decades. Yet because of their experience, they feel like they are in charge of the negotiation.

Now imagine Jerry starts making a concession that you—the observer—know is unnecessary. You must be able to call a time-out to reassess whether that concession was needed. This is the power of the time-out and the importance of an equal team, no matter the positions of everyone involved.

Call Prebriefs

A great time to review roles and responsibilities, the power of the time-out, and alignment on equality is during a prebrief. A prebrief is an internal conversation that takes place with your team before entering the discussion. It's an opportunity to review each person's role on the team, objectives of the negotiation, and why each role equals success for each negotiation. This last point is critical—if you want each person to do their job well, they must understand why they need to fulfill that role (and why they can't steamroll or perform others' roles).

It's also a great time to review success drivers, the range of acceptable outcomes, taboo subjects, and what you've uncovered during the research phase. You'll also brief the higher-ups that the negotiation is taking place and prepare them for the counterparty to potentially reach out.

It's common for the counterparty, after the first few negotiations, to circumvent you by reaching out to someone higher up the chain. This is a backdoor approach to try to get what they want. And oftentimes this strategy is incredibly successful because the team didn't prepare them for this to happen, and therefore they are taken by surprise. Perhaps they are even disappointed in their team, embarrassed, and willing to make the counterparty happy.

Remind leadership that this is a common tactic and assure them that it does not indicate that the negotiation is going poorly. It merely shows that your team is looking out for leadership's best interest. Remind them that they will receive negotiation summaries from the project manager to stay informed.

After someone on the team assures leadership that everything is going smoothly, you'll be busy preparing for worst-case scenarios.

Conduct Premortems

The premortem is an exercise created by Gary Klein as a method of prospective hindsight. Project the outcome of the negotiation in the future and look back.

A postmortem is when a coroner surgically or otherwise evaluates a cadaver to estimate the cause of death. In business, a postmortem is any evaluation of the efficacy of an initiative, project, task, or discussion. Did it fail? And if it did, why?

A premortem is similar in all ways except for the timing. A premortem forecasts the cause of death, or the reason why the negotiation failed (or where it could have been improved). To conduct this thought experiment, imagine it's six months in the future and the contract still isn't signed. Then ask the open-ended question, "What went wrong?"

Did someone on your internal team go rogue and accidentally sabotage your efforts? Are you stuck in a loop of concessions with diminishing returns? Did the counterparty go over your heads to make a deal with leadership? Was a certain success driver not met? Spend time running through the most likely scenarios. In doing so, you'll be better prepared to stop them from happening in the first place.

To conduct a successful premortem, you'll need to create an environment that celebrates radical honesty in your team. If someone doesn't feel confident that they can be honest about their teammates, the counterparty, or the deal itself, then the entire exercise is less effective.

After explaining why honesty is important, you can ease into this exercise by starting with the counterparty. Generally it's easier to locate flaws and problems externally, so start there. Review your influencer map of the counterparty. Who are the difficult people on their team? After a few negotiations, this part will become easier.

Next turn your gaze inward. Is there anyone on your team that you'll have to have separate conversations with to ensure that they fully understand what's expected of them? Is there anyone who might say something they shouldn't? Does anyone appear unable to fulfill their role?

Lastly, an essential element of a premortem is roleplaying with your team.

Roleplay

Roleplaying is the single most important thing you can do to get ready tactically before your negotiation. The entire purpose of this book is to teach you how to plan, prepare, and strategize.

But at some point in time, you have to actually discuss concessions and ask the questions on your question set. You can talk about martial arts all you want, but you can't enter your first match without practicing and sparring first.

Knowing a negotiation is in your future, it's critical that you practice doing these things *before* you enter the room. That's the only way to know how a question might land or to feel comfortable with your range of acceptable outcomes.

While conducting mock negotiations, pay attention to how you react. You want to uncover your strengths and weaknesses. What are you good at? What are your triggers? Do you have any odd habits? Do you ever lose your cool? Pay attention to what is going on internally.

When you roleplay with your team, make sure you all feel comfortable giving and receiving feedback. It's important that everyone understands that the goal isn't to make each other feel better, but instead is to locate areas of improvement. That being said, you must always be polite, courteous, and respectful. As long as you do that, you'll likely find that this becomes a fun experience.

But as fun as roleplaying can be, it can also be painful. The reason critique can hurt is because it's *true,* and the truth might be different from how we view ourselves. It can open wounds and feel really personal.

As difficult as it can be to receive criticisms, it can be even harder to give them. You likely respect and like your colleagues, which can make it hard to provide accurate feedback. If you and your team don't feel comfortable roleplaying, you might consider hiring an outside consultant. I personally work with a business coach to point out all of my areas of improvement because I trust him to be impartial.

The issue with roleplaying and hiring outside consultants is that they may not necessarily understand your business. You might be able to depend on them for feedback about how you present yourself, but you can't expect them to be able to conduct a premortem, for example.

It might be helpful for you and your team to pretend to be characters. For example, your team member might play the role of the steamroller, talking over you and trying to steer the conversation. Or they might play the role of the master manipulator, working to tear apart your team. Meanwhile, you can consider yourself as playing a role, too. Imagine yourself as the greatest negotiator of all time. What would this person say? How would they act? Give yourself permission to step into the shoes of an even better version of yourself.

CHALLENGE: Roleplay

For this challenge, you and your team will try roleplaying. Let's start with step one, choosing an identity.

Step One: Choose Your Identity

Create name tags so that everyone understands who they are in the exercise. Include internal roles, like negotiator, project manager, and observer. But also include outside roles from the counterparty. Did you locate any difficult people on the influencer map? Include them.

Internal Team:

"Negotiator"

"Project Manager"

"Observer"

Counterparty:

"Steamroller"

"Manipulator"

"Control Freak"

"Irrational Negotiator"

"Rational Negotiator"

Take turns playing each role. When playing the internal team roles, try to emulate the best version of each. When playing the counterparty roles, be as difficult as possible. The more practice you get with your team, the more prepared you will be on negotiation day.

Step Two: Conduct a Mock Negotiation

Now that roles are assigned, it's time to run through your first fake negotiation. Here is a loose framework to follow:

- Introduce yourselves
- Set the agenda
- Begin negotiations
- Discuss success drivers

- Make an offer
- Hear their counteroffer
- Begin managing asks and trading concessions
- Perform a debrief

In practice, the negotiation will likely take many meetings. But during roleplay, you'll have to move through each part of a negotiation quickly. Just keep in mind that the actual negotiation could take months to complete.

Step Three: Give Feedback

Always offer feedback that is polite, courteous, and respectful. Follow that rule and it's unlikely you'll create any internal animosity. But also make sure that your feedback is useful. Tell your teammates exactly how you think they could have better managed the situation. Then, accept any feedback on your feedback. For example, someone might say that your advice on avoiding their trigger was really helpful, and they'd like more of that advice in the future.

I mentioned triggers earlier. Common triggers are getting angry when the counterparty misbehaves. That's really what we all think of when we hear that word. When I was in procurement, I once told a client he was serving me low-grade dog food with his shit offer just to get a rise out of him (it worked).

But not all triggers involve anger or offense. Many people are triggered to feel badly about themselves. I once negotiated with a salesperson who wanted so badly to have a "win-win deal" that I could get whatever I wanted by telling them I was disappointed with what they were offering. They'd give a reasonable proposal, and I might say:

"Hey I've been meaning to ask, what's up with the new proposal? I like you, man, and I just don't get why you're screwing me like that."

"What do you mean?" they'd ask, their heart sinking.

"Well, you come in here asking for these kinds of prices, and I just thought we were on the same side."

The poor salesperson would feel so bad after that, they'd give me whatever I wanted.

Part of this exercise is about understanding where you and your team are open to manipulation. If you're a people pleaser, let your team know and ask someone, perhaps the observer, to watch out for that behavior. Or if you are easily riled up, ask someone with a level head to keep you grounded. Great teams rely on each other to fortify individual weaknesses with the strength of the team.

Step Four: Repeat

Conduct multiple rounds, trading roles as necessary. Have fun playing the counterparty and feel confident as you and your team work together and become tighter. If you do this regularly, you will truly become an unstoppable force.

…That is, if you actually do it. I know it can be hard to be vulnerable, especially with your colleagues. But if you really want to outperform everyone else, you've got to practice. Toss your teammates this book and ask them to read this section. Once everyone is on board, you'll see the exercise pay you back tenfold during your first negotiation.

Negotiations Ninja Chapter 8 Breakdown:

Secret #8: The key to avoiding massive screwups is to work with a team.

- In team-based negotiations, each member plays a crucial role to ensure success. The negotiator leads the discussion, the project manager handles documentation and task follow-ups, the observer focuses on high-level trends and body language, and the coach/advisor offers guidance and support from an external perspective.

- Often an unsung hero, the project manager is responsible for taking notes, following up on tasks, creating summaries, and providing written records. Their skills directly impact the strength of the resulting contract.

- Observers play a vital part in noticing subtle cues and high-level trends that may be missed by other team members. They focus on nonverbal communication and reactions to help guide the negotiation strategy.

- A coach or advisor offers valuable support and guidance from an external perspective. They can help the team navigate challenges and strategize effectively, utilizing their experience and knowledge.

- A team-based approach to negotiations can lead to better outcomes, as each member contributes their unique skills and perspectives to the process. However, it's essential to be aware of potential challenges in working with a team and address them proactively.

Preparation is the foundation for a successful negotiation. By understanding the needs and interests of both parties, conducting research, establishing objectives, and assembling a well-rounded negotiation team, you are setting the stage to meet your success drivers. The groundwork you've laid in this stage will prove invaluable in the next phase of the negotiation process.

At this point, you've spent hours researching, strategizing, and assembling your team, and now it's time to put your preparation into action. This next chapter will guide you through the initial stages of the negotiation process, from setting the tone and establishing rapport with the counterparty, to navigating the complexities of the negotiation itself.

It's day one of negotiations.

CHAPTER 9

DAY ONE OF NEGOTIATIONS

S he glances at her watch. *One hour 'til showtime,* she thinks. She ditches her running shoes by the front door, cues up her favorite song, hops in the shower, and throws on her best-fitting suit. Hair pulled back in a smart bun, a bit of makeup but not too much, and she looks the part. She then plants her feet firmly on the ground, shoulder-width apart. Her name is Amy Cuddy, and this is (probably) what she looks like when she goes into what she calls her "superwoman pose". According to her, she does this before every speech to enter the right mindset.

This is called **priming**, and it helps release positive endorphins and hormones into her body so that she feels a certain way before she does something important. I recommend you try something similar. Whether it's a favorite song, a light jog, a podcast—whatever it is, use it to help pump you up before negotiations. You want to enter the room at your best, so learn how to bring the best out of you. Bring positivity and confidence into your every stride.

Then walk through the door, because it's time to negotiate.

> **Secret #9:** Start your negotiation successfully by setting the first meeting up for success.

The First Meeting

The first meeting is so important. This is your first impression of the counterparty and their first impression of you. This meeting will set the tone for subsequent ones. The question is, will you set the right tone?

Conduct an introduction and establish rapport

Begin by introducing yourself and anyone else on your team in the room. Then spend a bit of time getting to know the counterparty.

An old-school sales tactic I hate is all about making the counterparty feel as uncomfortable and unwelcome as possible. Old movies show the keen negotiator setting up the room with only enough chairs for their team and nowhere for the counterparty to sit comfortably. Or they'll humiliate the counterparty by giving them chairs that are much smaller or shorter than theirs. Maybe they'll show up half an hour late or give the counterparty the wrong address so they end up late. This always makes the actor in the movie look powerful and cool. But in real life?

Stunts like that make you look like an ass.

Instead try to make the counterparty feel welcome and cared for. Make them feel comfortable. Ask whether you can bring coffee or tea. Make sure everyone knows where the bathroom is if the negotiations will be an hour or more. Ask what everyone does out of the office and learn whether you have common interests. Talk about a recent sporting event or popular movie. Go ahead and make small talk. It can feel weird to be so casual and informal after weeks of prepping and roleplaying, but remember, the only way that the counterparty will feel comfortable answering your questions and working with you is if they want to work with you and your team.

Once everyone is acquainted and comfortable, it's time to set the agenda.

Set the agenda

The agenda is a smooth transition between small talk and the actual negotiation. But aside from acting as that transition, it's also very practical. Review the meeting agenda that your project manager sent out to the counterparty for review weeks ago. Ask if there is anything they'd like to add or change. It's important to go through it, despite everyone having already read it. Why? Because it's possible the counterparty didn't actually read it at all.

Make sure to include a time limit and any scheduled breaks.

Then set the ground rules. Explain that if the discussion digresses, your project manager may interrupt to bring the conversation back on the rails. Ask if they agree that is the best approach (they will). Then establish how everyone will treat each other. Tell the counterparty that you will treat them with respect throughout the negotiation and ask that they treat you and your team the same. Stress how important collaboration is to you and your team. Explain that the project manager will send follow-up emails with important action items that need their approval. Emphasize the importance of getting back to each other in a timely manner. However you want the negotiation to go, outline it clearly.

Now you can move to the first point on your agenda.

Enter discussions

During the discussion part of a negotiation, both parties engage in a dialogue to exchange information, clarify their needs and interests, explore potential solutions, and build rapport. This phase is essential for understanding each other's goals and establishing a foundation for further negotiation. Here's what typically happens during the discussion phase:

- **Sharing information.** Each party shares relevant information about their needs, interests, and constraints. They may discuss their priorities, concerns, and any background information that could impact the negotiation.

- **Asking questions.** Both parties ask questions to clarify each other's positions, gather more information, and better understand each other's interests. Remember, open-ended questions can help uncover hidden concerns and stimulate creative problem-solving.

- **Active listening.** Listening carefully to each other's points of view is crucial for establishing rapport and gaining a deeper understanding of the other party's needs and interests. This involves being empathetic, attentive, and showing genuine interest in what the other party has to say.

- **Building rapport.** Establishing trust and a positive relationship is essential for successful negotiations. Both parties work to build rapport through open communication, respectful behavior, and finding common ground.

- **Identifying areas of agreement and disagreement.** Throughout the discussion, the parties identify points of agreement and disagreement. This helps them understand the scope of the negotiation and the areas where they need to work toward finding a mutually beneficial solution.

- **Brainstorming solutions.** Once the parties have a clear understanding of each other's needs and interests, they can start generating potential solutions. This may involve exploring various alternatives, finding areas of common ground, and discussing trade-offs or compromises.

- **Refining proposals.** Based on the discussion, both parties may refine their proposals and adjust their positions to better align with each other's interests. This process of give-and-take helps narrow down the options and move closer to a mutually acceptable agreement.

The discussion phase sets the stage for successful negotiation by allowing both parties to understand each other's interests, develop trust, and explore potential solutions. It is a crucial step in moving toward a mutually beneficial agreement.

The first debriefing

During the first debrief, review the project manager's notes with the team, include observations by the observer and negotiator, and make any adjustments needed. Review whether any items were left out and whether they need to be addressed at the next meeting.

Next, evaluate how the meeting went. Did you achieve what you set out to achieve? If you wanted to nail down price, do you have a number in front of you? If you didn't achieve your goal, why not? Further, what did your team do well? What did you do poorly? How can you do better next time? And once you ask those broad questions, inevitably you'll begin to prepare for the next meeting.

Prepare for the Next Meeting

In preparation for the next meeting, review the notes from your debriefing. If you identified major areas that need improvement, emphasize them in your next roleplaying session. Lastly, make sure you are continuing your counterparty research. What did you learn at the last meeting, and what do you hope to learn at the next? Get into the habit of continual research.

Practical considerations

Sometimes we can be so busy focusing on tactics and strategy, we forget practical considerations on the big day. Keep this basic advice in mind on game day.

Dress the part

Wear something professional that's going to create the right perception of you. I've seen a lot of people roll into negotiations virtually over Zoom or Teams in sweats. That's not going to be you. Instead, you're going to show up wearing something that fits the setting. If you are over Zoom, a button-up shirt or a sport coat is fine. If you're meeting in an industrial facility, khakis and a polo or blouse are fine. If you're meeting in the office, wear a suit. Look smart, but not over the top.

Eat light and sleep well

Just like an athlete before a big race, you want to eat breakfast but keep it on the light side. You don't want to eat a huge meal and feel sluggish or tired during the negotiation. If you'll be eating during the negotiation, steer clear of any messy foods. Sauces, finger food, pesto, and salads with large lettuce chunks are a few things to avoid. You don't want to start negotiating with basil in your teeth or a ketchup stain on your power suit. Oh, and get a good night's rest, too.

Do a priming exercise

Work out, listen to your favorite song, meditate, strike a power pose, or listen to a motivational podcast. Whatever your priming exercise is, make sure to build it into your schedule. You don't want to enter your negotiations late because your run lasted longer than expected.

What if Things Go Wrong?

In theory, we talk about negotiations in their ideal end state. But just because a negotiation should go a certain way—it should be straightforward or easy—that doesn't mean it's going to. We hope everyone will collaborate. We hope everyone will be professional and respectful. And we hope that we can sort out a deal in a reasonable amount of time.

We hope for those things, but that doesn't mean they will happen. There are a million things that could go wrong during this first meeting. It's important not to stress out preparing for the worst, but you do have to at least consider what you might do when things go off the rails. As I describe these worst-case scenarios, imagine yourself de-escalating.

What if the counterparty gets angry?

Do the opposite by remaining calm. Often we get angry because someone else is angry, and not necessarily because of the situation. When someone becomes reactive, stay neutral. It's usually in your best interest to de-escalate the situation.

Give the counterparty the opportunity to vent, and then employ a classic conflict resolution response: physically lean in, lower the pitch of your voice, speak more slowly, and try to label their emotion. Say something like, "It appears as though you might feel frustrated. Did I get that right?"

Keep in mind that they may have a legitimate reason to be frustrated that you are unaware of or haven't considered. But it could also be that you've uncovered an emotional trigger. Stay calm and make notes of what happened and why.

What if they have different expectations?

Sometimes the counterparty will take the negotiation in a totally different direction than the agenda you've just set. In this case, explore the tangent at the beginning of the negotiation because it's possible it should have been added to the list.

If there is no value to the discussion, either redirect them to the agenda or rely on your project manager to do so. If the counterparty seems agitated, ask them how important the topic is. Remain flexible and offer to discuss it at the next meeting.

What if I embarrass myself?

Own it. I've embarrassed myself so many times. Once I brought coffee in for everyone, but tripped and spilled it all over the table and on everyone's shirts. When you make a mistake, don't take yourself too seriously. Laugh it off and grab another coffee.

Made a bad joke that didn't land? Again, own it. Laugh, apologize, and say you thought it'd land better. Who knows, maybe everyone is just nervous. Sat down in a broken chair? Laugh and say you need to lose a few pounds. Got food on your shirt? Don't pretend it isn't there. Acknowledge it, make a little fun, and get back to business.

What if the counterparty is just totally unprepared?

It's a common misconception that if the counterparty is unprepared, they just don't care. But the fact that they sat down to negotiate with you proves that they do in fact care very much. If you complete every challenge in this book, you will enter your next negotiation 99 percent more prepared than anyone I've ever worked with, so by comparison everyone will start to seem unprepared. Instead of feeling insulted, recognize that you can use this to your advantage.

When the counterparty isn't prepared, they're likely to go along with whatever you say. So simply tell them about your "standard" contract that meets all of your success drivers. Who knows? They might just agree to all of it.

Alternatively, they could have been feigning ignorance or a lack of preparation as a tactic. Evaluate them based on what they do and the questions they ask, not what they tell you.

If they are genuinely unprepared and ask to reschedule, comply and be flexible but give them a few items to consider that meet your success criteria.

What if the counterparty uses strong-arm tactics or acts like a bully?

That's why you have a success framework—*use it*!

I don't care how manipulative, unyielding, or otherwise difficult the counterparty is, you can always rely on your success framework to ensure you get a deal that meets your success drivers. Most people who are strong-armed entered the negotiation unprepared in the first place—that won't be you.

If you know you'll negotiate with a bully, practice dealing with them during your roleplay. And make sure that the entire team reviews your success framework ahead of every negotiation.

What if the counterparty tries to take control of the conversation?

This is counterintuitive, but I want you to let them. Or at least let them feel like they are.

The reason I asked you to spend so much time evaluating how you present yourself, how you want to present yourself, how the counterparty presents, and how the counterparty wants to present is so that you can use that knowledge to your advantage.

The counterparty wants to be seen as a very powerful person? Fine, you're going to let them feel that way. You've got your success framework and you know you won't leave the deal without meeting your needs. Why not let the counterparty feel like they are in control?

When it's clear someone wants to control the conversation, I let them. I'll even use a quieter voice and allow them to go on tangents (within reason) that I normally wouldn't. I'll let them feel like they are a really savvy negotiator.

And by doing so, I open the door to them revealing things to me because they believe they have the upper hand. Someone wants to be the smartest person in the room? Let them be. Someone wants to be in control? Let them feel that way. Someone always gets what they want? Let them believe that they can have it.

On the flip side, if the counterparty clearly wants guidance, give it to them. If they want to be steered through the negotiation, by all means, take the wheel. Meanwhile, they're becoming your friend, not your competition. And your friends tell you their information.

What if the counterparty won't release information or fully answer your questions?

Then you've got a politician.

Sometimes people seem cagey because they don't know. Other times they don't believe you have a valid reason for wanting the information in the first place. Or maybe they believe the information is extraneous (and it very well may be).

First ask yourself whether you really need the answer. If so, explain to them why you need it. Show them that there is an incentive to give you that information, which might include a more profitable deal for everyone.

What if someone on your team says something they shouldn't?

TIME-OUT.

Call one!

However long you need to get back on the same team, take that time to refocus. If a team member calls a time-out on you, remember that you are on equal footing, and that it is their right. Listen to why they called the time-out and realign on objectives, roles, and responsibilities.

What if I get upset?

TIME-OUT.

Call another one!

Don't let the counterparty leverage your emotions against you. Take a moment to calm down, recalibrate, and reenter the negotiation when you're ready.

What happens if the right people aren't in the room?

When a decision-maker isn't in the room, you may have a problem. If you aren't sure whether anyone there can make a decision, there should be someone in the room who can strongly influence a decision. Ask what role the counterparty plays within the organization to determine whether they have decision-making authority or influence over the decision. If a decision-maker isn't present, ask whether they can be part of the discussion. At the very least, it may be possible to get them on the phone or through a web conferencing software.

What if I tend to be too empathetic?

Empathy is a wonderful quality in a person and in a negotiator. But many empathetic people allow themselves to let other people's needs get in their own way. Yes, the counterparty is in a tough position as this is the third time their child got into a fight at school, but they have to show up on time. Instead of allowing bad behavior, find out whether you can find a different time to meet, for example.

If you are too empathetic, lean on your team to balance you out. Ask them to help you manage expectations like deliverables and timelines so that the counterparty doesn't use your good nature against you.

What if I use absolutist language?

By absolutist language, I'm talking about when someone bluffs by saying something like "I can't go any further," or "This is the best I can do," when everyone knows they can. Based on the question, you've probably guessed that I don't recommend you ever use absolutist language (and yeah, I know that's an absolute statement, but there's always an exception to a rule).

How about this: try your best not to use absolutist language.

What's the big deal? As soon as you say "this is the lowest we can go," or "I can't go any further on the timeline," you back yourself into a corner. Ultimately, it eliminates flexibility. If you later realize that you would in fact go lower on price if other success drivers were met, then the counterparty either catches you in a lie and your ethos is shot, or you miss out on a better deal.

I'm not big on bluffing and I'm not big on people bluffing with me. It's dishonest, and more often than not, it decreases the overall value of the negotiation.

So back to the question…what if you slip up and make an absolute (and untrue) statement?

Roll it back. If you accidentally say, "That's the lowest I can go on price," quickly add something like, "that is, unless we can move some of these other metrics, like lengthening the term of the agreement." In this way, you show that you are flexible and potentially provision for another success driver.

To be clear, you can use absolutist language when it's true. I'm not big on dishonesty. If you really can't go any lower, say so. There is nothing wrong with telling the truth.

GO NEGOTIATE!

Armed with every secret uncovered, every challenge under your belt, and this field guide at your fingertips, you're ready for your first or next negotiation. If you've completed every exercise, you are going to absolutely wipe the floor with the counterparty.

But no matter how good you get—and I know you'll get really, really good—remember that negotiations are a practice, progression, and art. You'll learn something new with each new negotiation, and the rules are constantly changing.

Sometimes less is more. So as you move forward, I only ask you remember the following advice:

- A bad deal is often worse than no deal.
- Conflict isn't inherently bad.
- Preparation is everything.

I hope you are ready to get yourself more consistent results, reduce risk, and earn a hell of a lot more money. If you ever want to tell me about your most recent wins, you can find me at:

www.negotiations.ninja

Experts in Negotiation, Persuasion, and Conflict Resolution

Negotiations Ninja has brought together a team of leading experts in negotiation, persuasion, influence, and conflict resolution to ensure that it develops and delivers the most engaging training available.

If you want to take what you've learned in this book and put it into practice with the experts, find us at www.negotiations. ninja. Learn more about Negotiations Ninja by talking with our team and experience what so many leading brands have already experienced.

NEGOTIATIONS NINJA
PODCAST

You can find me hosting the *Negotiations Ninja* podcast, where we explore the strategies, skills, and mindsets of the world's top negotiators.

In each episode, we bring you interviews with experts from a wide range of industries and backgrounds, revealing their insights and tips for mastering the art of negotiation. Whether you're a seasoned negotiator or just starting out, you'll gain valuable knowledge and practical tools to help you achieve better outcomes in your negotiations. So join us as we dive deep into the world of negotiations and uncover the secrets of the best negotiators in the world. Visit https://negotiations.ninja/podcast/.

RECOMMENDED READING

This shouldn't be the only book on negotiations you read. The following titles explore a range of ideas. Some offer insight into areas I can't, like Eastern negotiation tactics and gender differences in negotiation. Others contradict my own beliefs—that's why I chose them. Negotiation isn't a religion, and I don't have all the answers. I hope you implement the strategies in this book, but I also encourage you to test them against other ideas and theories. Branch out and explore what other negotiation experts have to say. From a broad platform, you can fine-tune your abilities.

You Can Negotiate Anything by **Herb Cohen**

Herb Cohen is a man I deeply respect because of his understanding of how people may react and respond to different situations. I highly recommend this amazing book.

How to Win Friends and Influence People by **Dale Carnegie**

A classic! Dale Carnegie has inspired me for many years. And while the book seems old, the lessons in it have stood the test of time for generations.

The 7 Habits of Highly Effective People by **Stephen Covey**

While I don't agree with everything in this book, Covey has developed one of the most effective instructional books of our time. The value of this book lives on in the great training his company now carries out.

Getting to Yes: Negotiating Agreement Without Giving In by **authors Roger Fisher and William Ury**

Getting to Yes argues that win-win negotiations are not only possible, but what everyone should strive for. I disagree with many aspects of the book, but it is truly an amazing read. And you cannot discount the value that William Ury has contributed to the negotiation community. You have to read it!

Start with No by **Jim Camp**

The clearest anti-"getting to yes" book you will read. If you're looking for "the other side" of the negotiation spectrum, this book very clearly lays it out.

The Art and Science of Negotiation by **Howard Raiffa**

Howard Raiffa brought game theory into the negotiation world, and his contributions to the negotiation community should never be understated.

Chinese Business Negotiating Style by **Tony Fang**

In the introduction, I mentioned that this book is for western negotiations. If you're negotiating with organizations in the east, throw this book in the trash and read *Chinese Business Negotiating Style* instead. (I'm only half kidding because only half of what I teach will be relevant.)

The Kremlin School of Negotiation by **author Igor Ryzov**

This book offers a unique perspective on negotiation, drawing from the author's experience as a former KGB agent and a successful business negotiator. A must-read for understanding Eastern European negotiation styles.

Women Don't Ask: The High Cost of Avoiding Negotiation—and Positive Strategies for Change by **authors Linda Babcock and Sara Laschever**

Gender disparities and biases are real. Especially within negotiation. Read this book to learn more.

Influence: The Psychology of Persuasion by **Robert B. Cialdini**

What recommended reading list would be complete without recommending Cialdini? There's a reason he's viewed as the father of modern persuasion and influence. Read the book and find out why.

Human Hacking: Win Friends, Influence People, and Leave Them Better Off for Having Met You by **Christopher Hadnagy and Seth Schulman**

My friend, Chris Hadnagy, is a persuasive machine. There's a handful of people worth learning rapport building from. He's at the top of that list.

The Art of Seduction by **Robert Greene**

Robert Greene gives the blueprint to the psychological principles of seduction and how to attract and captivate others. A super fun read with tons of historical examples.

Rhetoric by Aristotle

The original master of persuasion. We're all standing on his shoulders.

The Only Sales Guide You'll Ever Need by Anthony Iannarino

I deeply respect Anthony Iannarino. He is so consistent and puts out instant classics. His work will last through the ages. Read this great book as a great starting point to his work.

The Book of Real World Negotiations: Successful Strategies from Business, Government, and Daily Life by Joshua Weiss

My friend Joshua Weiss is a brilliant thought leader in the negotiation community and has contributed so much that I feel awkward only calling out one of his amazing contributions. Want to read some great, real-life, negotiation case studies? Start with this.

The Jolt Effect: How High Performers Overcome Customer Indecision by Matthew Dixon and Ted McKenna

Matt Dixon's data-led work effectively illustrates why many sales don't convert. I absolutely love the work that Matt puts out. Start with this or *The Challenger Sale* to get a taste of his brilliance.

Stalling for Time: My Life as an FBI Hostage Negotiator by Gary Noesner

Gary Noesner is a personal hero of mine. After a life negotiating the most crazy situations, he now teaches others how to do the same. For a look into the life of a former FBI hostage negotiator, read this book.

Negotiation Hacks: Expert Tactics to Get What You Want by **Simon Rycraft**

Simon Rycraft is a brilliant negotiator and has distilled some amazing advice into an easy-to-use format in this incredible book. I consider him a friend and a role model.

The Trust Factor: Negotiation in Smartnership by **Keld Jensen**

Keld Jensen is a personal friend of mine who believes in trust and transparency in negotiations much more than I do. We agree on most things, but disagree sometimes on others. I respect him deeply. Read his books.

Negotiation Myth Busters: Rethinking Everything You Know about Building Strong Agreements by **Dan Oblinger and Allan Tsang**

These two are brilliant. We've had many conversations and debates that have ended in more questions than answers. They are two of a handful of people that I would call when I need someone to challenge an idea that I have about negotiation.

ACKNOWLEDGEMENTS

I would like to express my gratitude to the following individuals and groups, without whom this book would not have been possible:

- My book coach Michelle Stampe, who believed in this project and provided invaluable guidance and support throughout the writing process.
- My parents, who have always encouraged me to pursue my passions and supported me every step of the way.
- My role models, Dale Carnegie, Stephen Covey, Jim Rohn, Tony Robbins, Nelson Mandela, Teddy Roosevelt. You will never know how much you have inspired me.
- My friends, who have been a constant source of support and motivation, cheering me on through the ups and downs of writing.
- Members of the negotiation community, including Keld Jensen, Matt Dixon, Anthony Iannarino, John Barrows, Gary Noesner, Joshua Weiss, Simon Rycraft, Carson Heady, Herb Cohen, William Ury, Jim Camp, Allan Tsang, Tony Fang, Roger Dawson, and many

others for their expertise, inspiration, and contributions to the field.

- My business coach, Marty Park, for his guidance, encouragement, and accountability throughout my entrepreneurial journey.
- My podcast listeners and guests, for their support, feedback, and engagement, which has fueled my passion for sharing negotiation insights and strategies.
- All the amazing people who have taken my training and engaged with my social media posts, for their enthusiasm, curiosity, and willingness to learn and grow.

Thank you all for your contributions and support. I am deeply grateful for your presence in my life and for the role you have played in making this book a reality.

ABOUT THE AUTHOR

Mark Raffan of Negotiations Ninja is winner of several negotiation training awards who teaches multiple negotiation courses and has had a long career in procurement and sales. Born into a family of entrepreneurs, Mark always felt most at home when selling, negotiating, and managing conflict.

But the lure of entrepreneurship and the need to evangelize good negotiation practices became too great for Mark to ignore, and he decided to start a blog and podcast to evangelize great negotiation practices. The *Negotiations Ninja* blog and podcast were born.

They quickly began attracting readers and listeners from across the globe, and soon people began to reach out to Mark to provide training. The inbound requests became so great that Mark could no longer ignore these requests, and he decided to leave the corporate world to pursue the development of Negotiations Ninja full-time.

Negotiations Ninja quickly gained notoriety, grew very quickly, and has subsequently delivered training to some of the largest companies in the world in most major geographies, including North America, Central America, Europe, Asia, and Africa.

"I'm very fortunate to live and breathe negotiation, and I'm likely a bit odd because I believe that good negotiation skills truly have the ability to change people's lives."

— Mark Raffan, CEO of Negotiations Ninja

Manufactured by Amazon.ca
Bolton, ON

42388779R00118